the total
runner's
almanac

*the essential training tool and
information source for the runner*

Dr. Sharon L. Svensson

Published by The Trimarket Company, Palo Alto, California, USA

the total runner's almanac

the essential training tool and information source for the runner

by Dr. Sharon L. Svensson

Published by: The Trimarket Company
2264 Bowdoin Street
Palo Alto, California 94306
USA

Copy editor: Lauren Rusk, Ph.D., Stanford University

Illustrations by Susan Romero

Cover photo: Springtime Publishing AB

Other photos: Tony Svensson

Photo equipment: Canon EOS-1 and EOS-1n, EF28-80 mm f/2.8-4L USM, EF80-200 mm f/2.8L USM, EF70-200 mm f/2.8L Ultrasonic and, when necessary, Speedlite 540 EZ

Scans and color separations: Pixelmedia, Inc.

Production notes: This book was created using FrameMaker® from Adobe Systems, Inc. on Power Macintosh® and PowerBook® computers from Apple Computer, Inc. Art was produced using Illustrator® and photos edited using Photoshop® from Adobe Systems, Inc.

Printed and bound in the United States of America

ISBN: 0-9634568-9-X

Library of Congress ISSN: 1070-3306

First Edition published 1993. Second Edition 1997

Personal Information

If found, please return. This almanac contains information considered vital to its owner.

	Owner's name	
Winter	Street	
	City	
	State/province/country	
	Phone/fax/e-mail	
Summer	Street	
	City	
	State/province/country	
	Phone/fax/e-mail	
Best time and place to reach me		

	Running Gear	Size	Brand	Notes
Shoes	Training			
	Racing			
	Track			
Clothing	T-shirt			
	Running singlet			
	Shorts			
	Tights			
	Gloves			
	Warm-ups			
Other	Shades			

PLANNING CALENDARS

1997

January
```
S  M Tu  W Th  F  S
         1  2  3  4
 5  6  7  8  9 10 11
12 13 14 15 16 17 18
19 20 21 22 23 24 25
26 27 28 29 30 31
```

February
```
S  M Tu  W Th  F  S
                  1
 2  3  4  5  6  7  8
 9 10 11 12 13 14 15
16 17 18 19 20 21 22
23 24 25 26 27 28
```

March
```
S  M Tu  W Th  F  S
                  1
 2  3  4  5  6  7  8
 9 10 11 12 13 14 15
16 17 18 19 20 21 22
23 24 25 26 27 28 29
30 31
```

April
```
S  M Tu  W Th  F  S
       1  2  3  4  5
 6  7  8  9 10 11 12
13 14 15 16 17 18 19
20 21 22 23 24 25 26
27 28 29 30
```

May
```
S  M Tu  W Th  F  S
            1  2  3
 4  5  6  7  8  9 10
11 12 13 14 15 16 17
18 19 20 21 22 23 24
25 26 27 28 29 30 31
```

June
```
S  M Tu  W Th  F  S
 1  2  3  4  5  6  7
 8  9 10 11 12 13 14
15 16 17 18 19 20 21
22 23 24 25 26 27 28
29 30
```

July
```
S  M Tu  W Th  F  S
       1  2  3  4  5
 6  7  8  9 10 11 12
13 14 15 16 17 18 19
20 21 22 23 24 25 26
27 28 29 30 31
```

August
```
S  M Tu  W Th  F  S
                1  2
 3  4  5  6  7  8  9
10 11 12 13 14 15 16
17 18 19 20 21 22 23
24 25 26 27 28 29 30
31
```

September
```
S  M Tu  W Th  F  S
    1  2  3  4  5  6
 7  8  9 10 11 12 13
14 15 16 17 18 19 20
21 22 23 24 25 26 27
28 29 30
```

October
```
S  M Tu  W Th  F  S
          1  2  3  4
 5  6  7  8  9 10 11
12 13 14 15 16 17 18
19 20 21 22 23 24 25
26 27 28 29 30 31
```

November
```
S  M Tu  W Th  F  S
                  1
 2  3  4  5  6  7  8
 9 10 11 12 13 14 15
16 17 18 19 20 21 22
23 24 25 26 27 28 29
30
```

December
```
S  M Tu  W Th  F  S
    1  2  3  4  5  6
 7  8  9 10 11 12 13
14 15 16 17 18 19 20
21 22 23 24 25 26 27
28 29 30 31
```

1998

January
```
S  M Tu  W Th  F  S
             1  2  3
 4  5  6  7  8  9 10
11 12 13 14 15 16 17
18 19 20 21 22 23 24
25 26 27 28 29 30 31
```

February
```
S  M Tu  W Th  F  S
 1  2  3  4  5  6  7
 8  9 10 11 12 13 14
15 16 17 18 19 20 21
22 23 24 25 26 27 28
```

March
```
S  M Tu  W Th  F  S
 1  2  3  4  5  6  7
 8  9 10 11 12 13 14
15 16 17 18 19 20 21
22 23 24 25 26 27 28
29 30 31
```

April
```
S  M Tu  W Th  F  S
          1  2  3  4
 5  6  7  8  9 10 11
12 13 14 15 16 17 18
19 20 21 22 23 24 25
26 27 28 29 30
```

May
```
S  M Tu  W Th  F  S
                1  2
 3  4  5  6  7  8  9
10 11 12 13 14 15 16
17 18 19 20 21 22 23
24 25 26 27 28 29 30
31
```

June
```
S  M Tu  W Th  F  S
    1  2  3  4  5  6
 7  8  9 10 11 12 13
14 15 16 17 18 19 20
21 22 23 24 25 26 27
28 29 30
```

July
```
S  M Tu  W Th  F  S
          1  2  3  4
 5  6  7  8  9 10 11
12 13 14 15 16 17 18
19 20 21 22 23 24 25
26 27 28 29 30 31
```

August
```
S  M Tu  W Th  F  S
                   1
 2  3  4  5  6  7  8
 9 10 11 12 13 14 15
16 17 18 19 20 21 22
23 24 25 26 27 28 29
30 31
```

September
```
S  M Tu  W Th  F  S
       1  2  3  4  5
 6  7  8  9 10 11 12
13 14 15 16 17 18 19
20 21 22 23 24 25 26
27 28 29 30
```

October
```
S  M Tu  W Th  F  S
             1  2  3
 4  5  6  7  8  9 10
11 12 13 14 15 16 17
18 19 20 21 22 23 24
25 26 27 28 29 30 31
```

November
```
S  M Tu  W Th  F  S
 1  2  3  4  5  6  7
 8  9 10 11 12 13 14
15 16 17 18 19 20 21
22 23 24 25 26 27 28
29 30
```

December
```
S  M Tu  W Th  F  S
          1  2  3  4  5
 6  7  8  9 10 11 12
13 14 15 16 17 18 19
20 21 22 23 24 25 26
27 28 29 30 31
```

The 1999 calendar can be found on page 120

Contents

Preface

The Total Runner's Almanac is designed for, and by, runners. It is written by a dedicated long-distance runner, triathlete and duathlete. The author has been involved in US and international running and racing since 1981.

Since that time, numerous running books and training logs have been published. But there never emerged an easy-to-carry, useful and flexible source of personal training information until *The Total Triathlon Almanac* was introduced in 1992. It became an instant success among multisport aficionados. Then followed, specifically for the runner, the first edition of *The Total Runner's Almanac*. A run-away best-seller, this almanac struck a cord with runners all over the globe and quickly sold out.

Building on these books, what you're holding is the second edition of

the total runner's almanac

This new almanac has been left largely intact from the previous edition. The basic format, layout and design have remained the same and the logbook pages are still undated. Even the most diligent runner takes time off from training, whether voluntarily or not, and an empty-dated-page would often just cause extra anxiety. Better to skip the dates and make everybody look, and feel, better.

The almanac format is a series of separately contiguous right-hand and left-hand pages. The right-hand pages are weekly logs for you to keep. The left-hand pages comprise a training guide full of tips by expert runners and running authorities, interspersed by space to jot down your own plans, notes and key workouts.

Right-Hand Pages – *55 Week Running Log*
Each right-hand page is an undated running and training log that covers one calendar week. Use it as you'd like, but remember: you train to get fitter and faster, not to have the world's most awesome-looking logbook. The log can best help you monitor where you've been, where you are and where you're going if you keep your system simple.

Personalizing Your Log. There are two columns in which to record your running (many elite runners run twice a day) and three columns without captions for other types of aerobic activities, strength training and stretching. Some runners prefer to use the unlabeled columns for morning heart rates, hours and quality of sleep, weight and so on. One athlete uses the rectangular space around each day of the week to record how he feels on a scale of one to five. Another uses that space to note her weight before and after long runs,

Total Time

Date/Day	Run 1	~~Run 2~~				Notes
Mo 4/20/98	1.25 mi	19:47:00				Total miles done was 2 miles. Had to stop & turn around - rattlesnake in the middle of the road!
Tu 21	1.25 mi	25:00				Way too hot to have been running at 4:30 pm. Literally had to walk after 1.25 miles. Will try tomorrow to run in AM.
We 22	2 mi	21:01.58	5:35.64 5:23.76	5:47.07 5:15.11		Actually made it without stopping! AM run felt so much better than yesterday's disappointment. Rest tomorrow, AM run Friday & Saturday.
Th 23						REST
Fr 24	2 mi 21:26.64	5:26.8?	5:09.69	5:10.08	5:40.06	Does wind make a difference? Ran into wind 2nd mile. See what happens Saturday.
Sa 25						
Su 26						
Weekly Goal						
Weekly Actual						
Year To Date						

Notes

> *"The key to running faster is running faster."*
>
> The Author

Date/Day	Run 1	Run 2			Notes
Mo					
Tu					
We					
Th					
Fr					
Sa					
Su					
Weekly Goal					
Weekly Actual					
Year To Date					

particularly in hot weather.

Left-Hand Pages – *Training Guide and Notes*

The left-hand pages contain a series of support materials for runners of all ability levels and consist of a running handbook, cross training advice, a stretching program, tips from Olympic runners and running authorities, and four types of note pages.

Running Handbook. The first part of the training guide is the running handbook. It is divided into three phases, by fitness level. Among the many hints and guidelines for beginner and intermediate runners is an extract called "Rules of the Road" by the late, great George A. Sheehan, M.D., one of running's true gurus, on pages 28 to 29.

Cross-Training. After the third phase of the handbook is a brief section on cross-training for the runner, followed by the now famous stretching program. This section also provides definitions of lactic acid and the anaerobic threshold (AT).

Static Active Stretching. It's unlikely that you have seen anything like it before in a book for runners. The method, called static active stretching, was developed by Morris A. Mann, M.D. and used by several athletes on the tremendously successful 1988, 1992 and 1996 US Olympic teams. Recent evidence shows that stretching is of tremendous importance, particularly to the aging athlete. How you define "aging" is up to you; just remember that we stop growing somewhere around the 16th to 20th year of our lives. Although many of these stretching poses may appear yoga-like, they have been selected and developed further with the runner specifically in mind.

Your First Marathon. Running authority Joe Henderson has contributed "How to Train for Your First Marathon," which describes how the smart first-timer can prepare for this classic distance. You will learn an almost foolproof way to train, while minimizing the risk of injury.

Training Secrets of Elite Runners. Finally, there is a compilation of favorite workouts, including year-round training programs, from Midde Hamrin and Steve Scott. We chose these athletes because they provide different perspectives on running – from one long-distance, and one short- and middle-distance runner; one woman and one man; one European and one American. Both are experienced world-class runners and Olympic team members.

Key Workout Notes. Throughout the almanac are templates for specialized records of your key workouts. Based on input from many users and coaches, these note pages have been fine-tuned and now appear every other week (i.e., every other left-hand page is a

Date/Day	Run 1	Run 2				Notes
Mo						
Tu						
We						
Th						
Fr						
Sa						
Su						
Weekly Goal						
Weekly Actual						
Year To Date						

Key Long Distance Runs

Date	Split 1			Split 2			Overall			Notes
	Distance	Time	Pace	Distance	Time	Pace	Distance	Time	Pace	
1										
2										
3										
4										
5										
6										
7										
8										
9										
10										
Total		███		███				███		
Average										

Additional Notes:

Weekly Focus: _____   *Month & Year:* _____

Date/Day	Run 1	Run 2				Notes
Mo						
Tu						
We						
Th						
Fr						
Sa						
Su						
Weekly Goal						
Weekly Actual						
Year To Date						

note page). There are four different types of note pages, recurring in the following order:

- Notes
- Key Long Distance Runs
- Key Strength and Hill Runs
- Key Interval Runs

Many runners use these pages to expand on their experiences from the few key workouts of the week or month, or to plan for the future. Some of these note pages have quotes for added inspiration.

Appendix

The appendix contains information that may come in handy in the course of your training and racing year. You will find a rather comprehensive series of charts and templates to assist in four areas:

- Training
    - running overviews
    - interval running and pacing
    - cautions about heat and humidity

- Goal setting

- Race planning

- Record keeping (including US/metric conversion charts)

The charts and templates are further described in the appendix on page 121.

In the Next Almanac

Tell us! The almanac is developed for you, the runner. Although the methodologies described here have been tested and tested again by leading running authorities and fitness runners, as well as by some of the best athletes the world has ever known, they are not the last word. We want your feedback!

Weekly Focus: *Month & Year:*

Date/Day	Run 1	Run 2				Notes
Mo						
Tu						
We						
Th						
Fr						
Sa						
Su						
Weekly Goal						
Weekly Actual						
Year To Date						

Key Strength & Hill Runs

Date	Distance	Times Overall	Times Mile or km splits	Pace	Notes
1					
2					
3					
4					
5					
6					
7					
8					
9					
10					

Additional Notes:

Weekly Focus: *Month & Year:*

Date/Day	Run 1	Run 2				Notes
Mo						
Tu						
We						
Th						
Fr						
Sa						
Su						
Weekly Goal						
Weekly Actual						
Year To Date						

Running Handbook

This handbook can be used as a training and preparation guide for men and women interested in running or simply in maintaining above average fitness. The program is designed for people already engaged in some kind of fairly regular exercise. Before you begin to train, however, it is advisable that you heed this warning from the American College of Sports Medicine:

> At or above 35 years of age, it is necessary for individuals to have a medical examination and a maximal exercise test before beginning a vigorous exercise program. At any age, the information gathered from an exercise test may be useful to establish an effective and safe exercise prescription. Maximal testing done for men at age 40 or above or women age 50 and older, even when no symptoms or risk factors are present, should be performed with physician supervision.

Further prerequisites are that, *regardless of your age:*

- You are in good cardiovascular condition relative to the population and for your age
- You are familiar with your body's signals and can differentiate between a simple muscular ache or pain (caused by a hard training effort) and the more serious pain caused by a sprained or a strained muscle, tendon or ligament
- You get a thorough physical exam and obtain a physician's release

The program is divided into three phases: adapting to regular training; structuring your training into runs of various lengths and intensities; and integrating more advanced intervals.

Phase One: Training Adaptation

You first need to get mentally and physically used to a training regimen. Your cardiovascular system, muscles, joints, tendons and mind need time to adapt. There are no short cuts, though some individuals adapt more quickly than others. This phase lasts one month to one year, depending on your goals and your starting fitness.

Phase Two: Structure

Next you structure your training into hard and easy days. You also introduce long, slow distance (LSD) days. You may want to plan your longer run for the weekend and the hard days for during the week (since they demand less time). With the harder runs and your LSD runs, you will test your body to find out your strengths and weaknesses, and discover your tendencies for injury. *Listen to your body!* This phase lasts six weeks to six months.

Date/Day	Run 1	Run 2				Notes
Mo						
Tu						
We						
Th						
Fr						
Sa						
Su						
Weekly Goal						
Weekly Actual						
Year To Date						

Key Interval Runs

Date		Distance	Average Times		Number of Repeats	Notes
			Run	Recovery		
	1					
	2					
	3					
	1					
	2					
	3					
	1					
	2					
	3					
	1					
	2					
	3					
	1					
	2					
	3					
	1					
	2					
	3					
	1					
	2					
	3					
	1					
	2					
	3					
	1					
	2					
	3					
	1					
	2					
	3					

the total runner's almanac

Date/Day	Run 1	Run 2				Notes
Mo						
Tu						
We						
Th						
Fr						
Sa						
Su						
Weekly Goal						
Weekly Actual						
Year To Date						

Phase Three: Intervals and Integration

Finally, you introduce more advanced speed and interval sessions, further improve your skills, and prepare yourself for your first foot race. This phase tests your body at a more advanced level. Unless you are an elite runner, or otherwise very talented, this is a hard level to maintain over an extended period of time – but, it is extremely valuable to peak for the specific races that are really important to you.

TRAINING PRINCIPLES AND GUIDELINES

These principles and guidelines summarize the most important truths and wisdoms about running. We want you to *enjoy* running while staying fit, healthy and injury free. They are ideally combined with George Sheehan's "Rules of the Road."

1. Evaluate your present fitness level and set a realistic initial goal. Have a physician knowledgeable in sports,[1] particularly running, OK your proposed program.

2. Learn how to take your pulse (on the side of your neck just below your jawline or your wrist). Also, consider buying a heart rate monitor (particularly if you intend to go to phase three and beyond).

3. Keep a training diary or logbook, such as the one included in this book.

4. *Performance = Stress + Rest.* You train to maximize your race day performance. That is, you want to *maximize* all the parts of the above equation. In order to do so, you need hard and innovative training, as well as very serious rest. To learn when your body needs either is to learn how to train. Consequently, it is critical that you listen to your body at all times. If you are tired, rest, don't train! Learn to distinguish between the simple muscle discomfort that results from hard running and the more serious pain in joints, tendons and ligaments that may later cause injury. To decrease the risk of injury, develop and follow a hard/easy schedule. This means, for instance, that you *never* run hard, or long, on two consecutive days.

5. Do not increase your total weekly distance more than 10 percent per week.

6. If you get injured, back off. Go to a specialist in sports injuries (a good physician, chiropractor, or physical therapist). When you return to running, do not try to make up

---

[1.] Generally speaking, if your physician (or primary health care provider) is not into sports, chances are the advice and treatment you receive will be less than optimal for you, *from a runner's point of view.* This may sound like a controversial statement, but it's derived from my "Mom Principle": If your best friend's mom is considerably better at fixing pants, then you go to *her* rather than your own mom. Conversely, your friend is probably showing up at your house to sample *your* mom's wonderful apple pie.

Date/Day	Run 1	Run 2				Notes
Mo						
Tu						
We						
Th						
Fr						
Sa						
Su						
Weekly Goal						
Weekly Actual						
Year To Date						

Notes

> *"Free motion is free time."*
>
> Mark Allen
> On increased flexibility and running performance

Date/Day	Run 1	Run 2				Notes
Mo						
Tu						
We						
Th						
Fr						
Sa						
Su						
Weekly Goal						
Weekly Actual						
Year To Date						

for lost time; your body won't accept it. Start up gradually!

7. Warm up at the beginning of each run to decrease the risk of injury. Warm down at the end of each run to help speed recovery and prepare for your next run, even if it is a day or two away.

8. Stretch vigorously only after you run. Before running, do only very light stretching, if any: start every run very easily for five to ten minutes, stop to stretch if you like, and then resume your running.

9. Training depletes you. Eat a diet consisting largely of complex carbohydrates. Stay away from most fats (especially saturated fats) and simple sugars; take it easy on the animal protein. A common "sports diet" consists primarily of vegetables, grains, fruits, some dairy products and fish or poultry, though some athletes occasionally eat red meat and even blood products to ward off iron depletion. Other endurance athletes may eat read meat products several times per week during the heaviest phases of training and racing. Avoid processed foods; the fresher the food, the better. Supplement your diet with multivitamins, iron and vitamin C, if you like. Approximate percentages of caloric intake are listed below.

Carbohydrates	60 to 70 percent
Fats	15 to 20 percent
Protein	15 to 25 percent

10. Try to replace lost calories as soon after you train as possible.

11. Stay well hydrated before, during and after exercise. Most people tolerate water best, particularly in hot temperatures. There are many sport drinks on the market, some are better than others – experiment with them in training before using them in a race.

12. If you are on the road, run against traffic. And don't wear a Walkman! Madonna and Michael Jackson don't mix well with Traffic.

Date/Day	Run 1	Run 2				Notes
Mo						
Tu						
We						
Th						
Fr						
Sa						
Su						
Weekly Goal						
Weekly Actual						
Year To Date						

Dr. George Sheehan's Rules of the Road – I

1. Keep a record of your morning heart rate. Upon wakening and while still in bed, take your pulse. If you have a heart rate of five to ten (or more) beats higher than your morning norm, you have not recovered from your previous day's training or whatever stress you have exposed your body to. You may also be catching a cold or fighting off some other illness. Take the day off.

2. Weigh regularly. If you are overweight, you may not lose much weight initially – but soon you should lose up to one pound (half a kg) per week. Running consumes approximately 100 kilocalories per mile (~60 per km) and there are 3,500 kilocalories per pound (~7,000 per kg). The bigger you are, the more calories you consume.

3. Exercise daily. The more you run, the more muscle imbalance occurs. The calf, hamstring and lower back muscles become short, tight and inflexible. *They have to be stretched!* The shin, quadriceps and belly muscles become relatively weak. *They must be strengthened!*

4. Eat to run. Eat a good, high-protein breakfast, then a light lunch. Save the carbohydrates for the meal after the run to replenish muscle sugar.

5. Drink plenty of fluids. Water should be your first choice, but you can try any of the many sports drinks available. In hot and humid weather drink more! A good rule of thumb is to drink as much as your stomach can handle every 20 minutes, or so.

6. Run on an empty stomach. Run at least three hours after your last meal. Running causes increased peristalsis, cramps, even diarrhea. A bowel movement before running or racing may prevent these abdominal symptoms.

7. Wear the right clothes. In cold weather, wear many thin layers of clothing to protect against the wind and wet. In hot weather, wear light clothes, UV protective eye shades and a head covering.

8. Find your shoes and stick to them. If a shoe works, wear it. For training, you may want a heavier shoe with more cushioning, for racing a lighter shoe (e.g., a racing flat). Larger people need more cushioning and support.

9. Run economically. Do not bounce or overstride. You should lengthen your stride by pushing off, not reaching out. Do not let your foot get ahead of your knee. This means your knee will be slightly bent at footstrike. Run from the hips down with the upper body straight up and used only for balance. Relax.

10. Run against traffic. Face traffic. At night, wear some reflective material as close to the ground as possible.

Dr. George Sheehan's Rules of the Road – II

11. Belly-breathe. This must be practiced and consciously done just prior to a run or a race. Take air into your belly and exhale against a slight resistance. This helps prevent getting a "stitch."

12. Wait for your second wind. It takes about six to ten minutes and a one degree rise in body temperature to shunt the blood to the working muscles. When this happens you will begin to sweat lightly. Run slowly until this occurs, then put yourself on automatic pilot an enjoy!

13. Learn to read your body. Be aware of overtraining signs. If the second wind brings a cold, clammy sweat, head for home. Be alert to impending trouble. Loss of zest, light-headedness, scratchy throat, swollen glands, insomnia or palpitations are signs of trouble ahead.

14. Do not run with a cold. A cold may mean that you are overtrained or overstressed. Wait at least three days before you train again – take a nap the time you would have normally run.

15. Do not cheat on your sleep. Add an extra hour of sleep during heavy training periods. Take naps, if possible.

16. Be alert for signs of injury. Most injuries result with a change of training. A change in shoes, increase in weekly distance or intensity, hill work, and so on, are all factors that can affect your susceptibility to injury. Almost always there is some associated weakness of foot, muscle strength/flexibility imbalance, or one leg shorter than the other. Use of heel lifts, arch supports, orthotics, shoe modification and corrective exercises *(stretching!)* may be necessary.

17. When injured, find a substitute such as cross training. You want to maintain your fitness level. Swim, cycle or walk.

18. Training imposes stress on your system. The training cycle is stress-rest-stress. Your organism reacts to the stress, recovers and gets stronger during the rest, and is then ready for more stress. Each of us can stand different loads and needs different amounts of time to adapt. *You are an experiment of one.* Establish your own schedule; do not follow anyone else's. Listen to your body!

Editor's Note: Renowned running guru George A. Sheehan, M.D., is the author of Personal Best *and several other best-sellers on the life and philosophy of running. His new book,* Running to Win *describes how to find "the winner you," the winner inside you.*

Key Long Distance Runs

Date	Split 1			Split 2			Overall			Notes
	Distance	Time	Pace	Distance	Time	Pace	Distance	Time	Pace	
1										
2										
3										
4										
5										
6										
7										
8										
9										
10										
Total										
Average										

Additional Notes:

the total runner's almanac

Date/Day	Run 1	Run 2				Notes
Mo						
Tu						
We						
Th						
Fr						
Sa						
Su						
Weekly Goal						
Weekly Actual						
Year To Date						

EQUIPMENT

Buy only top-quality brand name shoes (there are about a dozen of those). Go to a running store staffed by runners and tell them you want a good shoe. Ask if the salesperson is a runner and what kind of running they do. Don't be timid – if they have first-hand experience with running, they will be delighted to spend time with you and introduce you to their running gear and accessory items.

They will ask you what kind of running you do (distance, surface, etc.) and analyze the characteristics of your gait (pronation, supination, heel striker, fore foot striker, and so on). The shoes you buy should be immediately as comfortable as bed room slippers yet give you the support your feet need based on your gait. If they don't feel exactly right don't buy them. For long distance running, they should be long enough to allow one thumb's width from your longest toe to the end of the shoe while you are standing. For shorter distances, this "rule of thumb" does not apply; you need slightly smaller shoes.

Aside from excellent shoes, the props needed for running are minimal. Wear what feels most comfortable to you, depending on the weather and your mood.

THE SCHEDULE

The three phases of your running schedule are detailed in the next three sections. Each phase serves as a preparation for the next. The sections describing them contain plenty of real-life advice and pointers. To avoid injury or burn-out, heed them well. You will find an overview of suggested running weeks for each phase in the appendix (page 122).

Phase One: Training Adaptation

Running places considerable stress on your body, so it's important to give your muscles and joints time to adapt. Your back, hips, legs and feet have to endure a pounding of many times your body weight over long periods; running on hard pavement or concrete only adds to this stress. Start out slowly; don't do too much, too soon!

First, you must *enjoy* the experience. It is hard to stick to a regular program that makes you miserable. Second, give yourself an incentive by setting a goal. (Remember, a realistic goal!) Select a foot race six weeks to three months down the road and develop a training plan for it. Both the 5 km (5 km = 5K = 3.11 miles) and the 10 km distances are good choices. Races are easy to find and challenging enough for people of all ability levels.

Start training by going out for 30 to 45 minutes two or three times a week. Separate your runs by at least one day of rest. Go out for a predetermined time, not distance. Jog a little, then walk a little at first, if you need to. Stay within your comfort zone. Find a pace at which you can carry on a conversation. If you push too hard, you may become injured

Date/Day	Run 1	Run 2				Notes
Mo						
Tu						
We						
Th						
Fr						
Sa						
Su						
Weekly Goal						
Weekly Actual						
Year To Date						

Key Strength & Hill Runs

Date	Distance	Times			Notes
		Overall	Mile or km splits	Pace	
1					
2					
3					
4					
5					
6					
7					
8					
9					
10					

Additional Notes:

Weekly Focus: *Month & Year:*

Date/Day	Run 1	Run 2				Notes
Mo						
Tu						
We						
Th						
Fr						
Sa						
Su						
Weekly Goal						
Weekly Actual						
Year To Date						

and, worst of all, you won't look forward to or enjoy the experience. *It is quite possible to enjoy running.* Most of those who say they hate it, probably push themselves too hard, beyond what's appropriate for their level of fitness. Nobody likes doing something that is painful or unpleasant.

It is also important to not worry about form, at this point – just relax and do what comes naturally. Every runner has an individual style that's as unique as his or her personality. Drop your shoulders and swing your arms loosely with your fingers relaxed. Look around, enjoy the day, and let your mind wander for a while. Then return to the task at hand and notice how your body feels.

After a while you will be jogging more and walking less. After three to six weeks, include some hills, but again, don't push too hard. Pace yourself and take the downhills easily. Listen to your body. When you are comfortable jogging along "indefinitely" you can try to run at an easy pace for one hour without stopping even though this may surpass your goal running time for most 5 km or even 10 km races.

Log your workouts: how much you ran, how much you walked and how you felt. Starting out at 30 minutes three to four times a week will give you a mileage base of about 12 miles (~20 km). Increase your mileage no more than 10 percent each week, otherwise you may injure yourself. Patience will pay off in the long run. If you have a partner who is a more accomplished runner, make sure that you do not let them determine your starting pace. Go easy!

Look ahead at where you'd like to be in one month, six months, one year, and so on. Use races to set goals for yourself. There are plenty of them around; they are great fun and a wonderful way to meet interesting, healthy people with priorities like yours.

When you have reached your goals in this phase and feel ready for more of a challenge, it's time to move on to phase two.

Phase Two: Structure

In this phase, your goal is to further develop your leg speed, strength and endurance. This involves three types of workouts. You do each once a week. You can also add one more day of running a week: a short, easy run, to avoid two consecutive hard or long workouts.

Leg Speed. The fartlek-type workout develops leg speed. (Fartlek is a Swedish word meaning speed play and it is just that: unstructured intervals of variable length and intensity.) After a five- to ten-minute warm-up, increase the pace or sprint for a short time, then jog again. Fartlek is unstructured: you vary your speed according to how you feel. Play with it. For instance, run harder between every other telephone pole or mailbox.

Weekly Focus: *Month & Year:*

Date/Day	Run 1	Run 2				Notes
Mo						
Tu						
We						
Th						
Fr						
Sa						
Su						
Weekly Goal						
Weekly Actual						
Year To Date						

Key Interval Runs

Date		Distance	Average Times		Number of Repeats	Notes
			Run	Recovery		
	1					
	2					
	3					
	1					
	2					
	3					
	1					
	2					
	3					
	1					
	2					
	3					
	1					
	2					
	3					
	1					
	2					
	3					
	1					
	2					
	3					
	1					
	2					
	3					
	1					
	2					
	3					

Date/Day	Run 1	Run 2				Notes
Mo						
Tu						
We						
Th						
Fr						
Sa						
Su						
Weekly Goal						
Weekly Actual						
Year To Date						

The total distance of this run should be four to six miles (6 to 10 km).

Strength. The "tempo run" develops strength. This hard, steady run should cover two to four miles (3 to 6 km), at a pace which you can maintain for that distance. Another strength workout is a hilly run at a brisk pace. As you approach a hill, get up on your toes and lift your knees. Push your arms down and back, and pump yourself up the hill. Run the downhills with short, quick steps. Your hips should lean forward and your body float (or almost fall) down the hill.

Endurance. The LSD run develops endurance. Most people save this run for the weekend. It should be approximately twice as long as your average run. Remember, never run any of these three (leg speed, strength or endurance) workouts on consecutive days. You need that easy day in between to recover.

Your Running Style. As you increase the intensity of your workouts, start monitoring your running style. Try to become more efficient. Look ahead about twenty feet (5 to 10 m). Relax your facial muscles and jaw; drop your shoulders. Swing your arms loosely at your sides and avoid crossing them over the body's centerline (this wastes energy). Your hands are cupped and relaxed (not clenched). All motion is forward, everything else is relaxed. Visualize the form of a good runner you admire and mimic that form. For long-distance running, a shorter, quicker, almost shuffling type of step is more efficient and less stressful. It is good form to land on the outside of the heel, roll inward and push off with the big toe. Changing your running form takes time. Be patient.

Cross-Training. If you'd like to experience the benefits of other types of physical activity, now may be a good time to do so. Turn to the "Cross-Training" chapter on page 52 to read more.

The workout variation of phase two makes your running more enjoyable as you prepare for phase three.

Phase Three: Intervals and Integration

You now run three or four times a week and have a more refined sense of speed and pace. You have been running for at least six months and are comfortable on steady runs of at least an hour. It is time to incorporate intervals of running at a harder-than-race pace for short distances interspersed by recovery (rest) intervals.

When you first introduce intervals, decrease your weekly mileage by about 10% so your body can adapt to the new stress. To begin with, do only one interval workout per week, in place of the fartlek run from phase two. Later on, you can restore the fartlek run to your program.

Date/Day	Run 1	Run 2				Notes
Mo						
Tu						
We						
Th						
Fr						
Sa						
Su						
Weekly Goal						
Weekly Actual						
Year To Date						

Notes

> "*Physical exercise is not merely necessary to the health and development of the body, but to balance and correct intellectual pursuits as well. The mere athlete is brutal and philistine, the mere intellectual unstable and spiritless. The right education must tune the strings of the body and mind to perfect spiritual harmony.*"
>
> Plato

Weekly Focus: *Month & Year:*

Date/Day	Run 1	Run 2				Notes
Mo						
Tu						
We						
Th						
Fr						
Sa						
Su						
Weekly Goal						
Weekly Actual						
Year To Date						

The main purpose's of interval running are to increase your leg speed and strengthen your heart muscle. This type of training also teaches you to run fast when your body is already tired and your muscles are under stress. You should perceive interval running as hard, but not impossible; the appendix on page 124 has more.

There are three basic ways to determine your recovery interval. First, you can take your pulse manually. Second, you can buy a heart rate monitor. And third, you can monitor how you feel. You don't want too little rest, because you want to finish each run evenly and in control, but you obviously don't want too much rest either.

If you use the heart rate method, you need to determine your maximum heart rate. A very general approximation is to deduct your age from 220. For a 30-year-old, we get 190 beats per minute (220 - 30 = 190). Assuming a maximum pulse of 190, you would elevate your heart rate to between 160 and 170 during each fast run, then let it drop below 120 before starting to run again.

If possible, use a track, or measure out one quarter to one mile on a flat road (or, on the metric system, measure out 500 to 1,500 m). On the track, run one-milers (four laps) or 1,500 m at the same pace (or faster than) you'd run a 10 km race. During these sessions, warm up by running slowly for about 15 minutes; then run three to four one-milers and walk up to one lap of the track for recovery between each mile. Then run slowly for 15 to 30 minutes to warm down. If possible, run intervals with friends; they are excellent motivators and can monitor your running form.

To prepare for shorter races, run half-milers (or 1,000 m) at the same pace you expect to run on race day. For instance, 10 km at 43:30 comes out to a mile pace of 7:00, and a kilometer pace of 4:21 (see the Conversion Charts & Figures, page 142). If you are running on a track, run two laps, and then walk half a lap. Gradually work up to four or five of these intervals all run at the same pace. Then run one mile or 1,500 m for time. If you have done your long runs at a decent clip and you can run a one-miler in considerably under 7:00, you can break 43:30 for a 10 km road race. The equivalent on the metric system is to run 1,500 m in less than 6:30.

Alternatively, run 440-yard intervals at about 1:40 to start with. After a few weeks, try eight 440s at 1:40 with 2:00 rest. Then you can start to cut your running times, but it's best to maintain the two-minute rest period for now. Using metric measurements, you would run 400 m a few seconds faster, but maintain the two minute rest period.

Intervals should not wipe you out. They are only a preliminary test, not the final exam. You should leave the track feeling pleased to have challenged yourself and confident that

Weekly Focus: *Month & Year:*

Date/Day	Run 1	Run 2				Notes
Mo						
Tu						
We						
Th						
Fr						
Sa						
Su						
Weekly Goal						
Weekly Actual						
Year To Date						

Key Long Distance Runs

Date	Split 1			Split 2			Overall			Notes
	Distance	Time	Pace	Distance	Time	Pace	Distance	Time	Pace	
1										
2										
3										
4										
5										
6										
7										
8										
9										
10										
Total										
Average										

Additional Notes:

Date/Day	Run 1	Run 2				Notes
Mo						
Tu						
We						
Th						
Fr						
Sa						
Su						
Weekly Goal						
Weekly Actual						
Year To Date						

you could do more if you had to. After only a few interval sessions, you will run more comfortably and efficiently at a quicker pace and be able to run faster while fatigued. This, in turn, will do wonders for your confidence; and confidence is essential to racing well.

For more specific interval running information, refer to the Interval Guidelines chart (page 124) and the two 10 km Interval Running & Pacing charts (pages 125 to 126). These three charts will help you put together appropriate track sessions in preparation for a 10 km road race. If you are running a marathon, figure out your average 10 km pace for the entire marathon and run your intervals at that pace. Also check out Joe Henderson's advice on pages 106 to 107.

Important: Although strictly speaking it's not necessary, many authorities strongly recommend the purchase and continuous use of a heart rate monitor at this stage and onwards. This is why: training effect is monitored by time, distance and intensity. Whereas it is possible to gauge intensity by perceived effort, there is a direct correlation between intensity and heart rate. Not only is this correlation more accurate than your perceived effort, it is easier to record, compile and analyze. If this argument does nothing for you, consider that many top endurance athletes use a heart rate monitor almost daily, particularly for their key workouts.

> *"I want to be thoroughly used up when I die, for the harder I work, the more I live. I rejoice in life for its own sake. Life is no 'brief candle' to me; it is a sort of splendid torch which I have got hold of for the moment, and I want to make it burn as brightly as possible."*
>
> George Bernard Shaw

Date/Day	Run 1	Run 2				Notes
Mo						
Tu						
We						
Th						
Fr						
Sa						
Su						
Weekly Goal						
Weekly Actual						
Year To Date						

Key Strength & Hill Runs

Date	Distance	Times Overall	Mile or km splits	Pace	Notes
1					
2					
3					
4					
5					
6					
7					
8					
9					
10					

Additional Notes:

Date/Day	Run 1	Run 2				Notes
Mo						
Tu						
We						
Th						
Fr						
Sa						
Su						
Weekly Goal						
Weekly Actual						
Year To Date						

Cross-Training

When you feel comfortable with the running load in the second phase, you may want to incorporate cross-training workouts in your weekly schedule. You've spent the first two phases learning and refining the fundamentals of running. Now is a good time to start integrating other types of training into your schedule.

Why Cross-Train?

You may ask why you should subject your body to activities that aren't directly related to running. After all, you want to become a fast, fit and efficient *runner,* and you can do without that other stuff. Besides, you may have a hard time fitting the running into your already busy schedule. Nevertheless, there are some very specific benefits to these alternative endorphin-chasing activities. Cross-training will help you:

• Prevent running-related injuries

• Recover from the stress of running

• Strengthen and balance muscle groups that are not used primarily for running

• Maintain high cardiovascular and musculoskeletal fitness in spite of injury

There are also some distinct drawbacks to cross-training – you might as well be aware of them up front. Cross-training might require that you:

• Master a new set of motor skills

• Acquire some new equipment

• Gain access to clubs and other facilities

Normally, cross-training consists of combination workouts, in which you go from one fundamental activity in a multisport event to the next. In the triathlon, for instance, you go from swimming to cycling, from cycling to running.

Cross-Training for Runners

The objective of your cross-training, however, is different than the duathlete's or the triathlete's. These athletes need to train their bodies to switch from one phase of their event to the next and to do it in one fluid motion with elevated, sometimes maxed-out, heart rates. You, however, may want to look at cross-training simply as a way to add variety to your running regimen, while gaining the physiological benefits discussed in the preceding section. Therefore, you can take the following approach:

• Normally, you cross-train only on the days you don't run.

Weekly Focus:　　　　　　　　　　　　　　　　*Month & Year:*

Date/Day	Run 1	Run 2				Notes
Mo						
Tu						
We						
Th						
Fr						
Sa						
Su						
Weekly Goal						
Weekly Actual						
Year To Date						

Key Interval Runs

Date		Distance	Average Times		Number of Repeats	Notes
			Run	Recovery		
	1					
	2					
	3					
	1					
	2					
	3					
	1					
	2					
	3					
	1					
	2					
	3					
	1					
	2					
	3					
	1					
	2					
	3					
	1					
	2					
	3					
	1					
	2					
	3					
	1					
	2					
	3					
	1					
	2					
	3					

Date/Day	Run 1	Run 2				Notes
Mo						
Tu						
We						
Th						
Fr						
Sa						
Su						
Weekly Goal						
Weekly Actual						
Year To Date						

- Should you wish to run and cross-train on the same day, run first. Running pounds your body more than most activities, and to start a run on already tired legs is something you're not likely to do in a race. Also, since running is your priority, it makes sense to run when you're physically fresh and mentally alert.

- Popular cross-training activities can be divided into two categories, those which yield either cardiovascular or musculoskeletal benefits. The cardiovascular category includes cycling, cross country skiing, hiking, rowing and swimming. The musculoskeletal group includes downhill skiing, strength training and stretching.

Most team sports (such as basketball, hockey, soccer, volleyball and water polo), while primarily cardiovascular, also require certain coordination and social skills.

If you are interested in learning more about cycling and swimming as cross-training activities, *The Total Triathlon Almanac – 1993* has several chapters for beginning, intermediate and advanced cross-trainers. These chapters are organized similarly to the running handbook in this almanac (pages 18 to 48), so you will quickly recognize your level. There's an order form on page 143 if you cannot find a copy at your favorite running or book store.

Injury Prevention and Management

Although you may never aspire to do a triathlon, you would probably benefit from acquiring some of the same skills as the triathlete. Specifically, if you do develop a running injury and you have cross-trained, you are already used to different types of physical activity. This enables you to "train through" what for many runners would be a debilitating injury. It's clearly an excellent way to prevent you from losing the fitness level you have worked so hard to gain. And mentally, it will make injuries far more easier to deal with. *The cross-training may even improve your running in the long term.*

If you want to learn more about stretching as a cross-training discipline and a way to prevent injuries, you should find the next chapter of interest.

Lactic Acid and the Anaerobic Threshold

Lactic acid: a substance which accumulates in your system during exercise and causes fatigue. The heavier the exercise, the more lactic acid is accumulated. Also often referred to as blood lactates.

Anaerobic threshold (AT): the intensity level at which your body is starting to accumulate lactic acid at a rate which your system can barely deal with. Beyond the AT, you are accumulating excess lactic acid. With proper training, you can improve your AT, and thus performance.

Date/Day	Run 1	Run 2				Notes
Mo						
Tu						
We						
Th						
Fr						
Sa						
Su						
Weekly Goal						
Weekly Actual						
Year To Date						

Notes

> *"Any world class marathoner that enhances his range of motion and lengthens his stride by one inch would break the two hour barrier."*
>
> Morris Mann, M. D.

Date/Day	Run 1	Run 2				Notes
Mo						
Tu						
We						
Th						
Fr						
Sa						
Su						
Weekly Goal						
Weekly Actual						
Year To Date						

Static Active Stretching –
Secret of the 1992 US Olympic Team

As you know, muscle fibers act by contracting. The longer they are, everything else being equal, the more they are able to contract. And a fiber that is old, inflexible or loaded with lactic acid does a poorer job than a fiber that is young, flexible or has less lactic acid. Volumes have been written to explain the benefits of stretching, but never as succinctly as the three illustrations below. The first illustration shows the effect of lactic acid on muscle fiber length:

NEGATIVE EFFECT OF LACTIC ACID

A young muscle fiber: ▬▬▬▬▬▬▬▬▬▬▬

A young muscle fiber saturated with lactic acid: ▬▬▬▬▬

The second illustration, below, shows how aging decreases muscle fiber length:

NEGATIVE EFFECT OF AGING

An older muscle fiber: ▬▬▬▬▬▬▬▬

An older muscle fiber saturated with lactic acid: ▬▬▬

And the third illustration, below, shows the positive effects of static active stretching:

POSITIVE EFFECT OF S·T·R·E·T·C·H·I·N·G

A stretched older muscle fiber *saturated with lactic acid:*

▬▬▬▬▬▬▬▬▬▬▬▬

Date/Day	Run 1	Run 2				Notes
Mo						
Tu						
We						
Th						
Fr						
Sa						
Su						
Weekly Goal						
Weekly Actual						
Year To Date						

Key Long Distance Runs

Date	Split 1			Split 2			Overall			Notes
	Distance	Time	Pace	Distance	Time	Pace	Distance	Time	Pace	
1										
2										
3										
4										
5										
6										
7										
8										
9										
10										
Total										
Average										

Additional Notes:

Weekly Focus: *Month & Year:*

Date/Day	Run 1	Run 2				Notes
Mo						
Tu						
We						
Th						
Fr						
Sa						
Su						
Weekly Goal						
Weekly Actual						
Year To Date						

Thus, an older and properly stretched muscle fiber can get longer than a young fiber, even when saturated with lactic acid. An optimally stretched muscle fiber will do the best job for you, lactic acid notwithstanding.

Now that you understand the importance of stretching, it's time to introduce the work of Morris Mann, M.D. The good news is that he's developed a complete stretching program which all you need to do is follow. The bad news is that it will be uncomfortable, at first. And you have probably heard that stretching should be comfortable and relaxing. Static active stretching, however, requires some discomfort to get the job done. Very simply, you will be pushing your body in many of these maneuvers. Without this discomfort, you will not reach the results your body is capable of.

The list of athletes who have successfully adopted Dr. Mann's static active stretching program is long. Each individual Dr. Mann has worked with personally has won a US national or World championship or an Olympic gold medal. Among the more well-known athletes are swimmer Pablo Morales (28), track runner Regina Jacobs (29), and triathletes Mark Allen (35) and Paula Newby-Fraser (31).

Pablo Morales

Pablo, winner of two medals in the 1984 Olympics, failed to qualify for the 1988 Olympics and stopped swimming for several years. While working as a coach for the Stanford Masters Team, he met Dr. Mann, one of his swimmers. Amazed by Dr. Mann's flexibility and wanting to give the Olympics one more try, Pablo adopted his method of static active stretching. Pablo took a year off from law school and began the journey back to Olympic shape. Swimming with the Stanford University team while following an extended stretching program designed by Dr. Mann, he qualified for the 25th Olympiad. Once in Barcelona, he did what almost everyone with a knowledge of swimming was hoping for, he won the gold in the 100 m butterfly. He also won the team gold in the 4 by 100 m medley. The "Old Soldier" had come back.

Regina Jacobs

Deserving an entire chapter of her own, Regina is a US national champion in the 1,500 m track and field event. Although she was a dedicated runner, while pursuing an MBA at the UC Berkeley in 1992 (one of the top business schools in the world), she simply could not give enough time to training. Attempting to follow through on a two-year academic program whose rigors are legendary, she had painted herself into a corner. But in the fall of 1991, she started training in earnest for the US Olympic qualifiers and began Dr. Mann's program. Nine months later, within three weeks, she both qualified for the Olympic Team and graduated with her MBA.

Date/Day	Run 1	Run 2				Notes
Mo						
Tu						
We						
Th						
Fr						
Sa						
Su						
Weekly Goal						
Weekly Actual						
Year To Date						

Key Strength & Hill Runs

Date	Distance	Times			Notes
		Overall	Mile or km splits	Pace	
1					
2					
3					
4					
5					
6					
7					
8					
9					
10					

Additional Notes:

Date/Day	Run 1	Run 2				Notes
Mo						
Tu						
We						
Th						
Fr						
Sa						
Su						
Weekly Goal						
Weekly Actual						
Year To Date						

Mark Allen

Known to his fellow athletes simply as "The Grip" (as in *the grip of death*), Mark is the best all-around triathlete the world has ever known. Being concerned about the accumulating effects of age and wear on his body, and having specific performance goals for his last years as a top competitor, he sought out Dr. Mann to help him with his flexibility. Mark noted that "This flexibility program has allowed me to transition quicker from the bike to the run, and to run more relaxed and efficiently, particularly towards the end of a race." He now feels more confident tackling the illusive eight-hour barrier for the Hawaii Ironman – the triathlon's version of a two-hour marathon.

Paula Newby-Fraser

Paula is a five-time winner of the Hawaii Ironman and the queen of long-distance triathlons. A former ballet dancer, she already knows the benefits of stretching for performance. Still, she has found Dr. Mann's approach of great value and is now working with him to improve her flexibility. She, too, has some very specific performance goals and wants to leave her competitive career with a Hawaii Ironman record that will stand for some time.

Proper Breathing for Static Active Stretching

In following the static active stretching program, breathing is critical. Proper breathing enhances control and allows you to extend into the maneuvers in a naturally gradual manner. According to Dr. Mann, "if you don't breathe right, you've got nothing." This is how you do it:

• Breathe through your nose and only through your nose.

• Take long, slow and deep breaths. Extend both the exhalation and inhalation.

• Constrict your epiglottis (more commonly known as the "wind pipe") until you make a slight hissing sound during both inhalation and exhalation. If you do it properly, there will be a continuous hissing as you inhale, a quiet moment, and then a continuous hissing as you exhale. The trick is to constrict your throat to the point where your epiglottis, not your nostrils, is limiting your air supply. So even though you breathe through your nose, the sensation you have is one of breathing with your throat. Most people get it right within seconds, once they learn how properly to constrict their epiglottis.

Important: read carefully the Tips on Doing it Right (page 72) before starting the maneuvers.

Date/Day	Run 1	Run 2				Notes
Mo						
Tu						
We						
Th						
Fr						
Sa						
Su						
Weekly Goal						
Weekly Actual						
Year To Date						

Key Interval Runs

Date		Distance	Average Times		Number of Repeats	Notes
			Run	Recovery		
	1					
	2					
	3					
	1					
	2					
	3					
	1					
	2					
	3					
	1					
	2					
	3					
	1					
	2					
	3					
	1					
	2					
	3					
	1					
	2					
	3					
	1					
	2					
	3					
	1					
	2					
	3					
	1					
	2					
	3					

Date/Day	Run 1	Run 2				Notes
Mo						
Tu						
We						
Th						
Fr						
Sa						
Su						
Weekly Goal						
Weekly Actual						
Year To Date						

Static Active Stretching –
Tips on Doing it Right

The stretching maneuvers can be done on the floor or a thin pad. You may find the standing maneuvers (Set 1) easiest to do on grass or the floor, and the others easiest on a thin pad.

1. Take off your shoes and socks, and wear clothing that allows freedom of motion.

2. Gradually extend into each maneuver with each exhalation. When you cannot extend further, stop! You will notice a certain level of discomfort at this point.

3. When you have completed the number of breaths required *or* you can no longer breathe through your nose as described earlier, stop doing the maneuver.

4. If you adhere to this program for a longer period of time (several months), you will experience the following benefits:

   • **3 times/week:** a definite improvement in your flexibility for as long as you stick with the program.

   • **4 times/week:** a *significant* improvement in your flexibility for as long as you stick with the program.

   • **6 times/week:** a *permanent* improvement in your flexibility, even *after* you stop the program. (If you stretch six days a week, take the seventh day off.) Choose your desired level of accomplishment accordingly!

5. Regardless of the level you wish to reach, take one day a week off.

6. Absolutely do not bounce! If you do, you will not gain the benefits of static active stretching and the bouncing may cause micro-tears in the muscles.

7. With time, you will notice that the discomfort is actually quite bearable, even relaxing and "centering." The key is to work into the full maneuver slowly and gradually.

Date/Day	Run 1	Run 2				Notes
Mo						
Tu						
We						
Th						
Fr						
Sa						
Su						
Weekly Goal						
Weekly Actual						
Year To Date						

Set 1 – Standing Maneuvers

These basic maneuvers provide general stretching of the body as a whole.

Maneuver 1 – The Forward Bend

With an exhalation, bend forward and attempt to place the fingers on the floor. If this is not possible, grab the ankles or wherever it is comfortable. Then, with each successive exhalation, extend your grip forward and then down. Never bend your knees. Try to bend from the waist. With each exhalation, extend forward until ultimately the head is on the knees. Hold this position for at least 10 to 15 breaths. With an inhalation return to the standing position. This maneuver stretches the hamstrings, the calves and the muscles in the lower back. It is a particularly useful stretching maneuver for a runner.

Maneuver 2 – Standing Forward Trunk Rotation

Stand in place. Spread the legs apart approximately 3 to 3 1/2 feet (about one meter). Turn the right foot 90° to the right, keeping the right heel in line with the left instep. Keep the left leg on the right and on the inside. Exhale. Bend the trunk sideways to the right bringing the right palm near the right ankle. If possible, the right palm should rest completely on the floor. Stretch the left arm up bringing it in line with the right shoulder and extend the trunk. The back of the legs, back of the chest and the hips should be in a straight line. Look towards the thumb of the outstretched left hand. Keep the right knee locked tight by pulling up the kneecap and keep the right knee facing the toes. Remain in this position for 5 to 10 breaths. With an inhalation, return to your starting position with legs spread apart. Turn the left foot 90° to the left, turn the right foot straight ahead. This maneuver stretches the trunk, the back and the hamstrings. It is particularly useful as a beginning maneuver for extending your stride.

Date/Day	Run 1	Run 2				Notes
Mo						
Tu						
We						
Th						
Fr						
Sa						
Su						
Weekly Goal						
Weekly Actual						
Year To Date						

Maneuver 3 – The Extended Leaning Right Angle

Spread the legs sideways 4 to 4 1/2 feet (about 1.3 meters). With a slow exhalation, turn the right foot 90° to the right keeping the right heel in line with the left instep, the left leg stretched and tight at the knee. Bend the right leg at the knee until the thigh and calf form a 90° angle and the right thigh is parallel to the floor. Place the right palm on the floor by the side of the right foot if possible, with the right armpit covering and touching the outer side of the right knee. Stretch the left arm out over the left ear and turn the head up. Remain in this position for 5 to 10 breaths, inhale and stand up. Repeat the maneuver on the other side. This maneuver is very helpful in stretching out the muscles of the back and chest. It is particularly useful after a long, hard run.

Maneuver 4 – The Standing Right Angle

Spread the legs approximately 4 to 4 1/2 feet apart. Exhale as you turn to the right and simultaneously turn the right foot 90°. Flex the right knee until the right thigh is parallel to the floor. The bent knee should be directly in line with the heel. Stretch out the left leg and tighten at the knee. Lift the head up; lift the arms up and join them at the palms. Try to have the nose directly in line with the thumbs. Hold this maneuver for 5 to 10 breaths. Stand up and repeat on the other side. This maneuver develops quadriceps strength, hamstring strength and lower back strength.

Date/Day	Run 1	Run 2				Notes
Mo						
Tu						
We						
Th						
Fr						
Sa						
Su						
Weekly Goal						
Weekly Actual						
Year To Date						

Key Long Distance Runs

Date	Split 1			Split 2			Overall			Notes
	Distance	Time	Pace	Distance	Time	Pace	Distance	Time	Pace	
1										
2										
3										
4										
5										
6										
7										
8										
9										
10										
Total										
Average										

Additional Notes:

Weekly Focus: *Month & Year:*

Date/Day	Run 1	Run 2				Notes
Mo						
Tu						
We						
Th						
Fr						
Sa						
Su						
Weekly Goal						
Weekly Actual						
Year To Date						

the total runner's almanac

Maneuver 5 – The Standing Right Angle With Arms Extended

Spread the legs approximately 4 to 4 1/2 feet apart. Raise the arms sideways in line with the shoulders and palms facing down. Turn the right foot 90° to the right. The left foot is kept static, keeping the right heel in line with the left instep. Keep the left leg stretched and tight at the knee. Stretch the hamstring muscles at the left leg. Exhale and bend the right knee until the right thigh is parallel to the floor. Stretch out the arms sideways as though you were being pulled by the fingertips from opposite ends. Turn the face to the right and gaze at the right palm. Hold this maneuver for 5 to 10 breaths. Stand up and repeat on the other side. This maneuver develops quadriceps and hamstring strength and causes a significant degree of tension on the lower back.

Set 2 – Back Strengthening Maneuvers

The lower back maneuvers are useful for all people and all sports. Only a rare individual has a strong lower back, in fact, most runners have experienced lower back pain at some point. The objective of these maneuvers is to eliminate this problem.

Maneuver 6 – The Bow Maneuver I

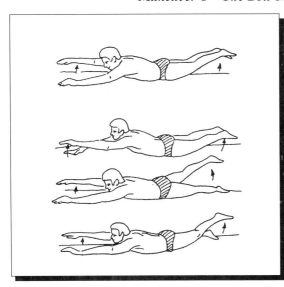

1. Lie down, arms and legs extended, belly and chest on the ground. With an exhalation, lift the right arm and both legs, making a bow in the lower back. Hold for 5 to 10 breaths. With an exhalation come down.

2. Lift the left arm and both legs, hold for 5 to 10 breaths, come down with an exhalation.

3. Repeat with both arms and right leg.

4. Repeat with both arms and left leg. Rest for 15 to 30 seconds.

5. Repeat with both arms and legs for 5 to 10 breaths *(not pictured)*.

This maneuver strengthens the lower back, which is particularly useful for hill running.

Date/Day	Run 1	Run 2				Notes
Mo						
Tu						
We						
Th						
Fr						
Sa						
Su						
Weekly Goal						
Weekly Actual						
Year To Date						

Key Strength & Hill Runs

Date	Distance	Times Overall	Mile or km splits	Pace	Notes
1					
2					
3					
4					
5					
6					
7					
8					
9					
10					

Additional Notes:

Date/Day	Run 1	Run 2				Notes
Mo						
Tu						
We						
Th						
Fr						
Sa						
Su						
Weekly Goal						
Weekly Actual						
Year To Date						

Maneuver 7 – The Bow Maneuver II

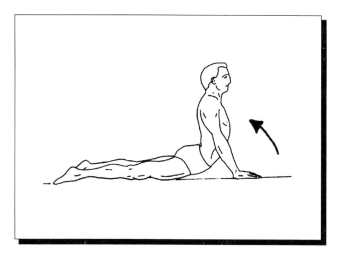

Lie down with the chest on the floor, place the thumbs together at the midline of the chest and push up, arching the back and lifting the head. Hold this maneuver with the legs and feet extended for 5 to 10 breaths. Come down and engage immediately in the next maneuver.

Maneuver 8 – The Bow Maneuver III

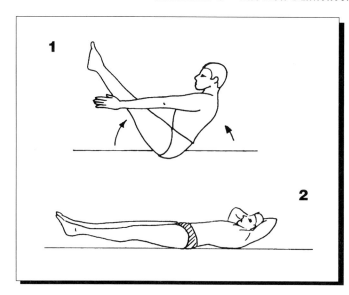

1. Lie on the back with the arms extended. With an inhalation, bend forward in the middle, developing a 45° angle between the chest and legs *(top graphic)*. Hold this position for between 15 and 45 seconds. With an exhalation, come down to the starting position and rest.

2. Clasp the hands together in the back of the head, lift the shoulders off the ground and bring the feet 6 inches (~ 15 cm) off the ground *(bottom graphic)*. Hold this position for between 10 and 30 seconds, then rest.

Date/Day	Run 1	Run 2				Notes
Mo						
Tu						
We						
Th						
Fr						
Sa						
Su						
Weekly Goal						
Weekly Actual						
Year To Date						

Key Interval Runs

Date		Distance	Average Times		Number of Repeats	Notes
			Run	Recovery		
	1					
	2					
	3					
	1					
	2					
	3					
	1					
	2					
	3					
	1					
	2					
	3					
	1					
	2					
	3					
	1					
	2					
	3					
	1					
	2					
	3					
	1					
	2					
	3					
	1					
	2					
	3					
	1					
	2					
	3					

Date/Day	Run 1	Run 2				Notes
Mo						
Tu						
We						
Th						
Fr						
Sa						
Su						
Weekly Goal						
Weekly Actual						
Year To Date						

Maneuver 9 – The Shoulder Stand

Lie flat on the back. Place the hands by the side of the legs, palms down. Exhale. Bend the knees, moving the legs toward the stomach until the thighs touch the stomach. Then raise the hips with an exhalation and raise the hands on the hips, bending the arms at the elbows. With an exhalation, raise the trunk further up into the perpendicular position, legs extended straight and trunk supported by the hands until the chest touches the chin. Only the back of the head and the neck, the shoulders and the back of the arms up to the elbows should rest on the floor. Clasp hands together in the middle of the spine and hold this position for as long as possible. Start with a minute and a half and extend by 15 seconds each day until you can do 10 minutes. Immediately following the shoulder stand, go into the next maneuver. Please note that there are several illustrations of the shoulder stand. All that has changed is the position of the hands.

About the shoulder stand: This is perhaps the most important maneuver to help low back pain or strengthen the lower back. The benefits to be gained from this maneuver, however, are entirely time dependent. The longer you can hold this position (up to 10 minutes), the more likely you will experience the benefits.

The maneuver develops the sacrospinalis musculature so it is readily visible.

After having finished the shoulder stand, it is particularly important immediately to go into the next maneuver, the plow. Do this once, and you will understand why.

Date/Day	Run 1	Run 2				Notes
Mo						
Tu						
We						
Th						
Fr						
Sa						
Su						
Weekly Goal						
Weekly Actual						
Year To Date						

Notes

> *"The marathon is magical. But the magic doesn't come without cost."*
>
> Joe Henderson

Weekly Focus:　　　　　　　　　　　　*Month & Year:*

Date/Day	Run 1	Run 2				Notes
Mo						
Tu						
We						
Th						
Fr						
Sa						
Su						
Weekly Goal						
Weekly Actual						
Year To Date						

Maneuver 10 – The Plow Position

With an exhalation, drop the legs from the perpendicular over the head to the point where the toes are on the floor immediately above and behind the head. Hold this position for exactly half the amount of time that you hold the shoulder stand, e.g., if you hold you shoulder stand for four minutes, hold the plow for two. The combination of these two positions tends to strengthen and stretch the lower thoracic region and the sacrospinalis muscula-

Set 3 – Sitting Maneuvers

Though any athlete can benefit from these stretches, these maneuvers are particularly useful for running.

Maneuver 11 – Sitting Forward Bend I

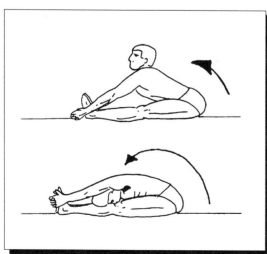

Sit on the floor with legs stretched straight in front. Place the palms on the floor by the sides of the hips. Exhale and extend the hands and grab your toes. Hold your big toes in each hand. Extend your spine and try to keep the back concave. When you start doing this maneuver, your back will be humped, because the spine is stretching only from the area of the shoulders. Concentrate on bending from the pelvic region of the back and extend the arms from the shoulders. Ultimately, the back will become flat and you'll be able to go forward very easily and place your face in between your knees. Keep your legs straight at all times.

Date/Day	Run 1	Run 2				Notes
Mo						
Tu						
We						
Th						
Fr						
Sa						
Su						
Weekly Goal						
Weekly Actual						
Year To Date						

Key Long Distance Runs

Date	Split 1			Split 2			Overall			Notes
	Distance	Time	Pace	Distance	Time	Pace	Distance	Time	Pace	
1										
2										
3										
4										
5										
6										
7										
8										
9										
10										
Total	■			■				■		
Average										

Additional Notes:

Date/Day	Run 1	Run 2			Notes
Mo					
Tu					
We					
Th					
Fr					
Sa					
Su					
Weekly Goal					
Weekly Actual					
Year To Date					

Maneuver 12 – Sitting Forward Bend II

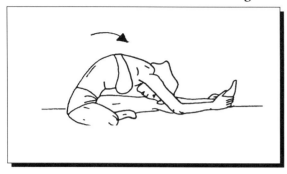

Sit on the floor with the legs stretched in front. Bend the right knee and move it to the left, placing the right heel against the inner side of the left thigh near the groin, specifically the perineum. The big toe of the right foot should touch the inner side of the left thigh. The angle between the extended left leg and the bent right leg should be a 90°. Stretch the arms forward and grab the left big toe with both hands. Lower the head to the trunk and then finally place your face upon your left knee. Hold for 5 to 10 breaths. Come up and repeat on the opposite side.

Maneuver 13 – Sitting Forward Bend III

This maneuver is similar to the previous one. Lift the left ankle onto the right thigh, thereby attaining a cross-legged position on that side. The knees should be at 90° relative to the outstretched leg. Grab your right big toe with both hands and lower your face to your knee, if possible. Hold for 5 to 10 breaths. Come up and repeat on the opposite side.

Maneuver 14 – Sitting Lateral Twist With Forward Bend

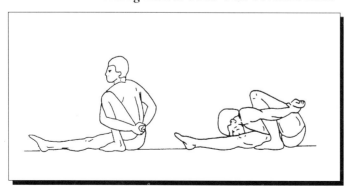

Sit on the floor with the legs stretched straight in front of you. Bend the left knee, placing the left foot flat on the floor. The shin of the left leg should be perpendicular to the floor and the calf should touch the thigh. Place the left heel near the perineum. The inner side of the left foot should touch the inner side of the outstretched right thigh. With an exhalation, rotate the spine as far to the right as possible. Rotate the left arm back around the uplifted knee and clasp both hands. Hold for 5 to 10 breaths. With each exhalation, try to bend further forward, finally placing the face on the right knee. Repeat this maneuver on the other side.

Weekly Focus: *Month & Year:*

Date/Day	Run 1	Run 2				Notes
Mo						
Tu						
We						
Th						
Fr						
Sa						
Su						
Weekly Goal						
Weekly Actual						
Year To Date						

Key Strength & Hill Runs

Date	Distance	Times Overall	Times Mile or km splits	Pace	Notes
1					
2					
3					
4					
5					
6					
7					
8					
9					
10					

Additional Notes:

Date/Day	Run 1	Run 2				Notes
Mo						
Tu						
We						
Th						
Fr						
Sa						
Su						
Weekly Goal						
Weekly Actual						
Year To Date						

Maneuver 15 – The Obturator Stretch

Sit on the floor with the legs stretched straight in front. Bend the knees and bring them close to the trunk. Bring the soles and heels of the feet together. Hold the feet together with the hands, locking the elbows in front of the knees, and with an exhalation, bend forward. With each exhalation, you should bend further forward until your face touches the floor in front of you and your knees touch the floor at right angles to your trunk. This maneuver stretches the inner muscles of the thigh.

Maneuver 16 – The Back & Quad Stretch

Step 1 (pictured): Kneel on the floor with your knees as close together as possible. Arch backwards and grasp your ankles with your hands. Deepen the arch in your lumbosacral area and attempt to look at your ankles.

Step 2 (not pictured): This is an extension of step 1 in which you spread your knees apart as far as possible. Then, with your hands on the floor lateral to the shins, attempt to slowly bring the back to the floor. Ultimately, the entire back is resting on the floor and the arms are extended horizontally, perpendicular to the trunk. This maneuver is particularly useful after a hard and hilly run.

The last maneuver: Many runners find it useful to once again do the forward bend (Maneuver 1).

Weekly Focus: *Month & Year:*

Date/Day	Run 1	Run 2				Notes
Mo						
Tu						
We						
Th						
Fr						
Sa						
Su						
Weekly Goal						
Weekly Actual						
Year To Date						

Key Interval Runs

Date		Distance	Average Times		Number of Repeats	Notes
			Run	Recovery		
	1					
	2					
	3					
	1					
	2					
	3					
	1					
	2					
	3					
	1					
	2					
	3					
	1					
	2					
	3					
	1					
	2					
	3					
	1					
	2					
	3					
	1					
	2					
	3					
	1					
	2					
	3					
	1					
	2					
	3					

Date/Day	Run 1	Run 2				Notes
Mo						
Tu						
We						
Th						
Fr						
Sa						
Su						
Weekly Goal						
Weekly Actual						
Year To Date						

How Static Active Stretching Will Maximize Your Potential as a Runner

There is a direct relationship between increased flexibility and enhanced performance. However, the musculoskeletal system loses flexibility quickly, probably somewhat more than one to two percent a year, starting as early as the age of 19. Still, you can adequately maintain your flexibility for years, and even improve it, with regular, specific training. The benefits of increased flexibility are

- Enhanced range of motion

- Reduced risk of injury

- More rapid recovery from combined physical stress (e.g., weight lifting and aerobic activity, such as running, on the same day)

- Increased ability of muscle fibers to generate force in spite of exposure to lactic acid

- Development of kinesthetic sense (awareness of, and sensitivity to, what your body as a whole is doing at any given time)

It is well known that athletes with greater flexibility tend to have more optimal performances and fewer injuries than those who merely have strength and endurance. Increasing your flexibility will allow you to optimize the strength and endurance you do have. The increased flexibility will enhance your range of motion – for example, by lengthening your stride in running – and will also allow you to recover more quickly between workouts.

Date/Day	Run 1	Run 2				Notes
Mo						
Tu						
We						
Th						
Fr						
Sa						
Su						
Weekly Goal						
Weekly Actual						
Year To Date						

How to Train for Your First Marathon

Joe Henderson

It took me almost ten years and more than 200 races to feel ready for my first marathon. And even then, it was the hardest work I'd ever done. So I still can't quite believe it when someone says, "I finished a marathon in my first year of running. And it was my first race of any type."

Thousands of people now do it that way. They're almost the majority at the first-timer-friendly Honolulu, New York and Stockholm Marathons. The effort is admirable – as long as this first try isn't the last. Sadly, I know dozens of people whose beginning was also their end. They failed in the attempt and decided it was too big a chore ever to try again. Or they succeeded in finishing and decided that once they'd been to the mountain top, why try again?

Marathon wanna-be's are tricky people to deal with. You don't want to put doubts in their head, yet you need to say, "Whoa, what's your hurry?" Take the case of a 37-year-old man named Mark from Washington, DC, who wrote to me in late December. This clearly was his New Year's resolution letter, though he didn't label it as such.

I can't call Mark a "runner" because he hadn't yet started to run when he wrote the letter. He was then walking an hour a day, six days a week, but had big plans. "I want to run the Marine Corps Marathon in 1993," he said. He'd outlined a program for the year that first transformed him from walker to runner, then increased his mileage to 60 a week by August, and finally added a two-hour run every weekend of September and October.

Mark asked me (and several other writers he'd addressed in this form letter), "Is this schedule too ambitious?" My reply: "I'm sure that a marathon is within your reach this year; if you don't sabotage yourself along the way. Injury, exhaustion and discouragement are the triple threats to all runners, and this is especially true for someone like you who is new to running. Yes, the schedule you've outlined is too ambitious. Hardly anyone trains 60-mile weeks for marathons anymore. The trend in marathon training is the opposite – to lower but more useful mileage.

I suggested a revised plan:

1. Set an initial goal that's shorter-term and shorter in length than the marathon. Concentrate on easing into running and then into racing, first by working up to an hour run and then by entering a 10-K race to sample that atmosphere which can intimidate a newcomer. Only at that point decide if the marathon is for you.

2. If it remains your goal, then de-emphasize miles per week to the point of not even counting them – run for time, not for miles. Instead, concentrate making the occasional long runs progressively longer and allowing plenty of recovery time in between them. Recover with three to five easy runs per week, none lasting longer than an hour.

3. Run long only once every two to three weeks, and make each of these runs longer than the one before. You might start at 1-1/2 hours, then go two hours the next time, then 2-1/2 and so on. Or you might advance by smaller steps.

4. Decide what your longest pre-marathon run will be. Some authorities say it should reach the full time you expect to take in the marathon. (For a rough estimate of that time, multiply your 10-K result by five.) I'm more conservative, suggesting only three-quarter-time training. For example, a four-hour marathoner can probably get by on a peak training run of three hours.

5. If these distances are a struggle to run in training, or if the marathon itself is, then try the "ultra-marathoners' trick" – take walking breaks. These walks have a magical effect in extending the distance you can cover. A sample ratio is run-15/walk-five.

"How does this plan work?" I wrote to Mark, anticipating his question. "I could fill a book with examples (many of them personal). But I'll just settle for one story. An organized marathon training group in Los Angeles follows a plan similar to this one. Nearly all of its members are first-time marathoners, and most are new runners. Last year, more than 500 people from this group started the L.A. Marathon. All but two of them finished."

Editor's Note: Joe Henderson, a longtime editor and columnist with Runner's World, also publishes the newsletter Running Commentary. *Subscriptions: $18 a year from 61 West 34th Avenue, Eugene, OR 97405.*

Training Secrets of Elite Runners

There are so many incredible elite runners that to select only a few to consider as models is an overwhelming task. Unless you pick 100 runners, you are sure to miss some of the best athletes in the world. To some degree, choice boils down to personal preference. Trying to appeal to the largest possible spectrum of runners, I chose Midde Hamrin (37) from Sweden and Steve Scott (37) from the United States.

MIDDE HAMRIN

Midde was an international caliber basketball player who came to the United States on a basketball scholarship, where she fell in love with running and her running coach, Andy Senorski. Under his tutelage, she became one of the best all-around runners Sweden has ever had. At one point in her career, she held the Swedish record in all distances between 5,000 m and the marathon. She is a two-time Olympian.

Her 14 years of running is marked by great successes as well as nerve-racking interruptions that brought her running to a standstill. She's had achilles tendon surgery and knee surgery, and has borne two sons. Every runner can learn from her comebacks, each time at a higher level and with new personal bests.

Coming Back

After the two surgeries, Midde didn't resume running until her health care providers gave permission. First, she ran very easily on soft surfaces no more than 30 minutes a day. She gradually added strength and flexibility training. After a few weeks with no problems (except the feeling that she would *never* get in shape ever again), she increased the distances. At about six weeks, she added a second run and tested light intervals. When all went well, she continued to build her base and interval load until she was ready to try a small 5 or 10 km race.

After childbirth, she followed the same steps, but with considerably less anxiety – there was no fear that the injury might return. She started a basic abdominal strengthening program a few days after the birth. Five weeks after her first son, Midde tried running, but it was too early. Her advice to other mothers is: "Don't begin until you feel it's right, but remember that running is a great way to relax from the demands of motherhood." After a total of six weeks, she was ready to resume her running: "By that time I wanted to train very badly. I almost started climbing the walls and was very happy to begin my running."

During her first pregnancy, Midde was able to keep up a light running program until the eighth month. With her second child it was different: "My body said stop to normal run-

Date/Day	Run 1	Run 2				Notes
Mo						
Tu						
We						
Th						
Fr						
Sa						
Su						
Weekly Goal						
Weekly Actual						
Year To Date						

ning already after the fifth month, so I began running in the pool with a 'wet vest' five times a week." Training with the wet vest (for running in deep water with a special type of floating harness or life vest – also called an "aqua jogger") allowed her to retain some of her conditioning, despite the layoff from running.

She has a tendency to get iron depleted and has found that controlled levels of iron supplements work very well, both during pregnancy and when she trains particularly hard. During long runs, she'll bring a water belt with a sports drink.

Midde and Andy feel that the key to her success is consistency over a long period of time and sticking to the basics. To her, that means mileage with long runs and long intervals. Short intervals are added as a final touch after the base has been established.

Base Training. Her base training is pretty much the same year round, weather permitting. Table 1 outlines her primary workouts. Monday through Friday she also runs approximately 10 km every morning (it's part of her morning routine, like brushing her teeth). This brings her total distance for a base training week to approximately 170 km, or 110 miles. No more than 15% is high-intensity work, such as intervals.

Day	Primary Run	Notes
Mo	Easy	~15 km
Tu	Intervals	8 - 10 x 1000 *or* 6 x 1,500 m
We	Pace	14 - 16 km
Th	Distance	18 - 25 km
Fr	Light	10 km easy
Sa	Fast distance	8 - 16 km (some hills)
Su	Long distance	30+ km

Table 1: Midde's base training

The Competitive Season. Midde likes to do intervals on the track, rather than fartlek or tempo runs: "On the track I always know exactly where I stand, which is great for race planning. It also puts some pressure on me to keep the quality up." She knows that when she completes a good set of long intervals, she is ready to race. For her, that would be 8 to 10 by 1,000 m on an average of 3:11 with 1 to 2 minutes' rest. (Midde's PR for the 10 km is 31:57 – compare with the metric interval chart on page 125.) Her primary workouts are listed in Table 2. Monday through Thursday she also runs her 10 km morning run. In contrast to her base training, Midde's competitive season training has higher

Date/Day	Run 1	Run 2				Notes
Mo						
Tu						
We						
Th						
Fr						
Sa						
Su						
Weekly Goal						
Weekly Actual						
Year To Date						

quality interval workouts and her weekly distance drops to 150 km, or less.

Day	Primary Run	Notes
Mo	Easy	~15 km
Tu	Long intervals	800 - 2,000 m
We	Pace	14 - 16 km
Th	Short intervals	200, 300 and 400 m
Fr	Easy	6 - 8 km, no evening run
Sa	Race	
Su	Intermediate distance	20 - 25 km

Table 2: Midde's competitive season training

Race Peaking. Midde likes to race often, particularly the 10 km and half marathon. Nevertheless, she does peak for a few races every year, such as the annual track meet between Sweden and Finland, and the European Championship. For a race of this magnitude, she'll take a two-week perspective, replace the weekend race with long rest intervals, and mix in lighter and shorter runs.

Days Before Race	Interval and High Intensity Runs	Notes
14	10 km road race	32:45
10	Long intervals	10 x 1,000 m (3:11 average, 2 min rest)
7	Short intervals	10 x 400 m (no time, 2 min rest)
4	Easy intervals	4 x 800 m (2:26 average, 4 min rest)
0	Race	31:57 (first place and Swedish record)

Table 3: Midde's race peaking

Table 3 shows her interval load the two weeks before she ran her most recent 10 km PR (this was in June 1990, 13 months after her first son was born).

The Future. Midde recently gave birth to her second child and finds herself once again on the road to a comeback. Though she is primarily known for her 10 km and half marathon times, she's an excellent marathon runner, having won the Chicago Marathon and

Date/Day	Run 1	Run 2				Notes
Mo						
Tu						
We						
Th						
Fr						
Sa						
Su						
Weekly Goal						
Weekly Actual						
Year To Date						

placed second in Boston. She feels that the marathon may ultimately be her best event and would like to improve upon her seven-year-old 2:33 PR with a sub-2:30.

STEVE SCOTT

Steve is the most successful miler this country has ever had. Steve has the most sub- 3:50 miles of anyone (eight) and still has the American record of 3:47.64. He won a silver medal in the World Championship in 1983 and has run 136 sub-4 miles. His 10 km PR on the roads is 28:22, and his best half marathon time is 1:03. 32 (on a hilly course).

He doesn't feel blessed with the same raw speed as some competitors, but believes he is a stronger runner who can endure a long season. At 37, he has been racing at world-class level for over 15 years, and plans to continue. Says his long-time friend and present coach Irv Ray, "Steve has this insatiable appetite for running and hard work."

He considers himself past his prime but still competitive at the world-class level: "I'm waiting for my 40th birthday." The many years of world-class running have given him an experience base that runners of all ability levels can learn from.

Structuring The Year

Steve divides his year in half and each half into three phases. The first half starts in September, the second in March. September consists primarily of long steady runs. In early October, he adds strength and hill work, as well as longer intervals. By the end of December (his first transition phase into speed), he mixes in shorter intervals for the indoor racing season. March is again a month of strength build-up and by April (his second transition phase into speed) he prepares for the higher intensity shorter intervals in May and June, to build to the June-July peak.

Strength & Endurance Build Up – I. The September base, with an average weekly distance of 90 miles and a longest run of 15 miles, provides the all-important foundation for the ensuing high intensity lifestyle of a versatile middle- and long-distance runner. The other runs are five to ten miles long, all at a comfortable pace.

Adding Intervals – I. In early October he adds what he calls endurance intervals. These are longer intervals, primarily mile repeats or 1,200 m at a 1,000 m pace (see Table 4). Early on he runs the mile repeats at 4:50, and as he gets in shape he gets down to 4:30. This prepares him for cross-country and 10 km road races.

Serious Track Work – I. By the end of December, Steve's weekly mileage rarely exceeds 90 miles, and he is doing shorter intervals at a pace of 60 seconds per quarter, or faster. This prepares him for the indoor track season, though he rarely attempts to peak this

Date/Day	Run 1	Run 2				Notes
Mo						
Tu						
We						
Th						
Fr						
Sa						
Su						
Weekly Goal						
Weekly Actual						
Year To Date						

Day	Run	Notes
Mo	AM: 5 mi easy PM: 6 x 1 mi (4:35 ave) 4 - 5 min jog in between each	total distance 15 miles
Tu	AM: 5 miles easy; PM: 10 miles brisk	
We	10 mi good pace	
Th	25 x 200 m hills hard + 5 miles out and back easy	total distance 13 miles
Fr	10 miles easy	
Sa	AM: 10 miles; PM: 5 miles	
Su	7 miles	Weekly total: 88 miles

Table 4: A week of Steve's November running

early in the year: "I wouldn't sacrifice too much for the indoor season." During this period Steve travels and races every other week or so.

Strength & Endurance Build Up – II. In early March, Steve is so fried from all the racing and travelling that a month of base work is a welcome interruption: "I need to work on my strength and add up the miles again." March's training is similar to September's.

Adding Intervals – II. In April it's back to intervals again. While maintaining some of the longer intervals from earlier in the year, he now primarily runs 800s and 1,000s (but all the intervals are faster than they were in October). In early April his 800 times are around 2:05, the following week they're down to 2:02, and the next they're 2:00. Because of the emphasis on speed, entire workouts may consist of no more than two miles of intervals.

Serious Track Work – II. In May it's time for even shorter stuff. Now he runs 57 to 58 minute quarters. The total high-quality portion of an entire workout may be no longer than one and a half miles. He tries to maintain his weekly mileage around 70 to 80 miles, but will cut down the intensity in preparation for the Nationals in mid June (see Table 5). Then it's off to Europe for a month of intense racing: "In Europe you're racing every two to five days. Your life consists of racing and jogging."

In other words, there is no time for quality training, just races, recovery from races, and preparations for the next one. His total weekly mileage during this racing phase has historically been 70 to 80 miles. Says Irv Ray: "With what we know today, we wouldn't mix long and short runs like this. I would try to get Steve to run no more than 50 miles weekly." Instead, his runs now emphasize low mileage, racing and jogging, strides, and a lot more rest.

Weekly Focus: *Month & Year:*

Date/Day	Run 1	Run 2				Notes
Mo						
Tu						
We						
Th						
Fr						
Sa						
Su						
Weekly Goal						
Weekly Actual						
Year To Date						

Day	Run	Notes
Mo	AM: 5 miles, PM: 5 miles both at comfortable pace	
Tu	AM: 5 miles brisk; PM: 5 miles easy	
We	3 (400 - 300 - 200) m; 3 mi jog before and after	total distance 12 miles
Th	8 - 10 miles easy	
Fr	5 miles easy	
Sa	Race: sub 3:50, first place	
Su	10 miles easy	Weekly total: 70 miles

Table 5: An ideal week of Steve's peak running

His Wednesday run is a key workout. After the three-mile warm-up, he runs 8 by 110 m strides (with spikes). His run times for the main set typically are 56 - 42 - 27, 54 - 41 - 27, 50 - 41 - 24. The recovery between each run is an easy 200 jog. In April, this is a different interval session, one Steve calls a transition (into speed) workout. This transition workout starts out with longer intervals and ends with a set of 400s as described in Table 6. He runs the same type of intervals in November.

Halfway through the summer racing season, Steve likes to go home for a few weeks to build up strength again, with what he calls a "mini-build-up." He runs easy 80 mile weeks and picks one interval workout weekly from his peak schedule. Then it's back to Europe for a few more weeks of the same. The season ends in August. He takes one or two weeks off and then starts back with the next year's strength and endurance build-up.

Interval	Time	Recovery
2 x 1,000	2:33, 2:33	400 jog
800	1:59	400 jog
3 x 400	59 ave	200 jog
2 (600 + 400)	1:28 & 59 ave	200 & 400 jog
3 x 400	58 ave	200 jog
4 x 200	26 ave	200 jog

Table 6: Steve's transition intervals

Weekly Focus: *Month & Year:*

Date/Day	Run 1	Run 2				Notes
Mo						
Tu						
We						
Th						
Fr						
Sa						
Su						
Weekly Goal						
Weekly Actual						
Year To Date						

The Future. In Irv Ray's words "Due to nagging overtraining, Steve has not been as consistent the last several years, but he still runs well and feels he can run competitively on the world track scene." He turned 40 in May 1996 and would now like to start breaking Masters records.

1999

	January			
S	M Tu W Th F	S		

January
```
S  M Tu  W Th  F  S
               1  2
 3  4  5  6  7  8  9
10 11 12 13 14 15 16
17 18 19 20 21 22 23
24 25 26 27 28 29 30
31
```

February
```
S  M Tu  W Th  F  S
    1  2  3  4  5  6
 7  8  9 10 11 12 13
14 15 16 17 18 19 20
21 22 23 24 25 26 27
28
```

March
```
S  M Tu  W Th  F  S
    1  2  3  4  5  6
 7  8  9 10 11 12 13
14 15 16 17 18 19 20
21 22 23 24 25 26 27
28 29 30 31
```

April
```
S  M Tu  W Th  F  S
                1  2  3
 4  5  6  7  8  9 10
11 12 13 14 15 16 17
18 19 20 21 22 23 24
25 26 27 28 29 30
```

May
```
S  M Tu  W Th  F  S
                   1
 2  3  4  5  6  7  8
 9 10 11 12 13 14 15
16 17 18 19 20 21 22
23 24 25 26 27 28 29
30 31
```

June
```
S  M Tu  W Th  F  S
       1  2  3  4  5
 6  7  8  9 10 11 12
13 14 15 16 17 18 19
20 21 22 23 24 25 26
27 28 29 30
```

July
```
S  M Tu  W Th  F  S
                1  2  3
 4  5  6  7  8  9 10
11 12 13 14 15 16 17
18 19 20 21 22 23 24
25 26 27 28 29 30 31
```

August
```
S  M Tu  W Th  F  S
 1  2  3  4  5  6  7
 8  9 10 11 12 13 14
15 16 17 18 19 20 21
22 23 24 25 26 27 28
29 30 31
```

September
```
S  M Tu  W Th  F  S
          1  2  3  4
 5  6  7  8  9 10 11
12 13 14 15 16 17 18
19 20 21 22 23 24 25
26 27 28 29 30
```

October
```
S  M Tu  W Th  F  S
                1  2
 3  4  5  6  7  8  9
10 11 12 13 14 15 16
17 18 19 20 21 22 23
24 25 26 27 28 29 30
31
```

November
```
S  M Tu  W Th  F  S
    1  2  3  4  5  6
 7  8  9 10 11 12 13
14 15 16 17 18 19 20
21 22 23 24 25 26 27
28 29 30
```

December
```
S  M Tu  W Th  F  S
          1  2  3  4
 5  6  7  8  9 10 11
12 13 14 15 16 17 18
19 20 21 22 23 24 25
26 27 28 29 30 31
```

Appendix

This appendix has a series of charts and templates to assist in four areas:

- Training (pages 122 to 129)
  - running overviews
  - interval running and pacing
  - effects of heat and humidity

- Goal setting (pages 130 to 133)

- Race planning (pages 134 to 135)

- Record keeping (pages 136 to 142)

1. Training: There are two Running Overview templates, the General with recommended training for the three phases described in the training handbook and the Personal. Use the personal one to plan your own running, say, over a season or before important races. There are also two interval running charts (10 km Interval Running & Pacing), one metric and one according to the US system of measurement, with guidelines.

There are three charts to help you understand the dangers of running in hot and humid climates. The first of the two Apparent Temperature charts is in degrees Celsius (°C), the second is in degrees Fahrenheit (°F). These two charts show the combined impact of relative humidity (in percent) and the environmental temperature as measured by a thermometer (in °C for the metric world and °F for others). The subsequent Heat Stress Risk chart explains the danger of physical activity in more detail.

2. Goal Setting: At a minimum, you can use these templates for your seasonal goal setting. The first, named Personal Best & Time Trial Record, is a rather comprehensive framework which enables you to set goals and compare your progress throughout the year. There are two of these charts, with and without pre-typed distances. The former is labelled Standard Distances, the latter is labelled Personal Favorite Runs and is for your favorite time trials or races, whatever distances they may be. It is unlikely that you will fill completely both, or even one, of these templates in a year's time. The Races – Goals & Actuals chart is pretty straight forward: before the race you plug in your goals, and after the race your actuals. *Then ponder the difference.*

3. Race Planning: The two blank Races To Do templates are self-explanatory.

4. Record Keeping: This section starts with two Race Record templates that can be used to compare your performance in races. Next are two Annual Summary templates (with guidelines), one by quarter, or your own chosen portion of the year, and one by week (which you can also divide further). Finally, there's a blank grid, called Annual Chart, for plotting distances or hours trained and physiological values. The exhibit on page 142 will help you convert between the metric and US systems of measurements, if necessary.

Please remember that all US and international copyright legislation apply.

RUNNING OVERVIEW – GENERAL

		Phase One	Phase Two	Phase Three
Objectives		Build confidence Learn skills	Differentiate your runs Increase intensity and volume	Further differentiate your runs. Improve skills Prepare for first race
Duration		4 weeks to 1 year	6 weeks to 6 months	6 weeks and on
Daily Run Range	**Metric [km]**	3 - 12	6 - 15	8 - 25+
	USA [miles]	2 - 8	4 - 10	5 - 15+
Runs/Week		3	4	5 - 6+
Weekly Run Range	**Metric [km]**	10 - 25	30 - 45	45 - 80+
	USA [miles]	5 - 15	20 - 30	30 - 50+
Comments		Add one run per week near the end of phase one	Always take a day off after your long or your hard run	Decrease your weekly run distance by 10% for the first several weeks when starting intervals

RUNNING OVERVIEW – PERSONAL

Objectives								
Duration								
Run								
Daily Range								
Sessions/Week								
Run								
Weekly Range								
Comments								

the total runner's almanac

INTERVAL GUIDELINES

The four variables of interval running are:

- Distance
- Run time
- Recovery time
- Number of repeats

On the next two pages are two Interval Training and Pacing charts for an individual preparing to run a 10 kilometer foot race. The first one is based on the metric system and the second one on the mile (for some US runners).

The charts are provided for the more accomplished runner who would like to design his or her own interval workouts. They give approximate values for each of the above four variables based on your actual race performance time. Please note that this is your *current* performance as opposed to your personal best or record (PR).

10 KM INTERVAL RUNNING AND PACING
metric system of measurement

Actual Race Performance			Training Interval Sessions								
Splits			2,000 m			1,000 m			400 m		
			Times		Number of	Times		Number of	Times		Number of
Overall Time	km	400 m	Run	Recovery	Repeats	Run	Recovery	Repeats	Run	Recovery	Repeats
50:00	5:00	2:00	9:40-10:05	5 min	3	4:50-5:00	4 min	6	1:48-1:53	3 min	8
48:00	4:48	1:55	9:20-9:40	5 min	3	4:40-4:50	4 min	6	1:45-1:50	3 min	8
46:00	4:36	1:50	9:00-9:20	5 min	3	4:25-4:35	4 min	6	1:40-1:45	3 min	8
44:00	4:24	1:46	8:30-8:50	5 min	3-4	4:15-4:25	4 min	6	1:36-1:40	2 min	9
42:00	4:12	1:41	8:10-8:30	4 min	3-4	4:00-4:10	4 min	6	1:32-1:36	2 min	9
40:00	4:00	1:36	7:40-8:05	4 min	3-4	3:50-4:00	3 min	6-8	1:28-1:32	2 min	9
38:00	3:48	1:31	7:20-7:40	4 min	3-4	3:40-3:50	3 min	6-8	1:25-1:30	2 min	10
36:00	3:36	1:27	6:50-7:15	4 min	3-4	3:25-3:35	3 min	6-8	1:18-1:22	1.5 min	12
34:00	3:24	1:22	6:30-6:50	3 min	4-5	3:15-3:25	2 min	6-8	1:12-1:14	1.5 min	12
32:00	3:12	1:17	6:00-6:25	3 min	4-5	3:05-3:15	2 min	6-8	1:08-1:10	1.5 min	14
30:00	3:00	1:12	5:40-6:05	3 min	4-5	2:50-3:00	2 min	8-10	1:04-1:07	1 min	16
28:00	2:48	1:07	5:20-5:40	3 min	4-5	2:40-2:50	2 min	8-10	0:58-1:02	1 min	16

the total runner's almanac

125

10 K INTERVAL RUNNING AND PACING
USA system of measurement

Actual Race Performance			Training Interval Sessions												
Splits			One Mile			Half Mile			Quarter Mile						
Overall Time	Mile	Quarter Mile	Times		Number of Repeats	Times		Number of Repeats	Times		Number of repeats
			Run	Recovery		Run	Recovery		Run	Recovery	
50:00	8:03	2:01	7:45-8:05	5 min	3	3:50-4:00	4 min	6	1:48-1:53	3 min	8
48:00	7:43	1:56	7:30-7:45	5 min	3	3:40-3:50	4 min	6	1:45-1:50	3 min	8
46:00	7:24	1:51	7:15-7:30	5 min	3	3:30-3:40	4 min	6	1:40-1:45	3 min	8
44:00	7:05	1:46	6:50-7:05	5 min	3-4	3:20-3:30	4 min	6	1:36-1:40	2 min	9
42:00	6:45	1:41	6:30-6:40	4 min	3-4	3:10-3:20	4 min	6	1:32-1:36	2 min	9
40:00	6:26	1:37	6:15-6:25	4 min	3-4	2:55-3:05	3 min	6-8	1:28-1:32	2 min	9
38:00	6:07	1:32	5:55-6:05	4 min	3-4	2:50-2:55	3 min	6-8	1:25-1:30	2 min	10
36:00	5:48	1:27	5:35-5:50	4 min	3-4	2:40-2:50	2 min	6-8	1:18-1:22	1.5 min	12
34:00	5:28	1:22	5:15-5:30	3 min	4-5	2:30-2:35	2 min	6-8	1:12-1:14	1.5 min	12
32:00	5:09	1:17	4:55-5:10	3 min	4-5	2:20-2:25	2 min	6-8	1:08-1:10	1.5 min	14
30:00	4:50	1:12	4:35-4:50	3 min	4-5	2:10-2:15	2 min	8-10	1:04-1:07	1 min	16
28:00	4:30	1:08	4:20-4:30	3 min	4-5	2:00-2:05	2 min	8-10	0:58-1:02	1 min	16

APPARENT TEMPERATURE*
in degrees Celsius (°C)

		Environmental Temperature [degrees Celsius]										
		20	25	27	30	32	35	38	40	43	45	50
Relative Humidity [%]	0	17	22	23	26	28	31	33	34	37	38	43
	10	17	22	24	27	29	32	35	37	41	43	48
	20	18	23	25	28	31	34	37	40	44	48	55
	30	18	24	26	29	32	36	40	44	51	56	65
	40	19	24	26	30	34	38	43	50	58	65	
	50	20	25	27	31	36	42	49	56	66		
	60	20	25	28	32	38	46	56	64			
	70	20	26	29	34	41	51	62				
	80	21	27	30	36	45	58					
	90	21	27	31	39	50						
	100	21	28	33	42							

*what it feels like to the body

Source: National Oceanic and Atmospheric Administration and by courtesy of Bob Talamini, The Houstonian Triathlon Club – *adapted*

the total runner's almanac

APPARENT TEMPERATURE*
in degrees Fahrenheit (°F)

		Environmental Temperature [degrees Fahrenheit]										
		70	75	80	85	90	95	100	105	110	115	120
Relative Humidity [%]	0	64	69	73	78	83	87	91	95	99	103	107
	10	65	70	75	80	85	90	95	100	105	111	116
	20	66	72	77	82	87	93	99	105	112	120	130
	30	67	73	78	84	90	96	104	113	123	135	148
	40	68	74	79	86	93	101	110	123	137	151	
	50	69	75	81	88	96	107	120	135	150		
	60	70	76	82	90	100	114	132	149			
	70	70	77	85	93	106	124	144				
	80	71	78	86	97	113	136					
	90	71	79	88	102	122						
	100	72	80	91	108							

*what it feels like to the body

Source: National Oceanic and Atmospheric Administration and by courtesy of Bob Talamini, The Houstonian Triathlon Club.

the total runner's almanac

HEAT STRESS RISK
in °C and °F

Apparent Temperature		Heat Risk
Celsius	**Fahrenheit**	
32 - 40	90 - 105	*Heat cramps or exhaustion possible*
40 - 54	105 - 130	Heat cramps or heat exhaustion likely Heatstroke possible
54+	**130+**	**Heatstroke highly likely**

How to use the APPARENT TEMPERATURE and HEAT STRESS RISK charts:

1. Check the outside temperature (say that it's 38°C, or 100°F).

2. Check the outside relative humidity (say that it's 60 percent).

3. Read off either of the two large apparent temperature charts (in our example you get 56°C, or 132°F).

4. Check off the small Heat Stress Risk chart on this page (in our example you get *"heat stroke highly likely"*).

5. In other words, if it's 38°C, or 100°F, outside and very humid, you are at a very high risk of getting heatstroke if you go for a run. This is dangerous to your health. Worse, it may *set back your training* for days, weeks or forever!

6. Another excellent way to observe your body's reaction to heat is to use a heart rate monitor. If your heart rate goes up above your target heart rate, stop and walk.

Source: National Oceanic and Atmospheric Administration and by courtesy of Bob Talamini; The Houstonian Triathlon Club – *adapted*

the total runner's almanac

PERSONAL BEST & TIME TRIAL RECORD – I

Standard Distances	All Time Personal Best		Time Trial Times											
	Time	Date	Preseason		Early Season		Peaking 1		Late Season		Peaking 2			
			Goal	Actual	Goal	Actual	Goal	Actual	Goal	Actual	Goal	Actual		
Time Trials														
400 m														
1,500 m														
1 mile														
3,000 m														
5 km/3 miles														
8 km/5 miles														
5 km														
10 km														
15 km														
Races														
10 miles														
Half Marathon														
Marathon														
50 km/miles														
100 km/miles														

Note: Although this is a grid of most meaningful time trial and racing distances, it is unlikely that you will fill out the entire chart in the course of a training and racing year.

the total runner's almanac

PERSONAL BEST & TIME TRIAL RECORD – II

Personal Favorite Runs	All Time Personal Best		Time Trial Times										
			Preseason		Early Season		Peaking 1		Late Season		Peaking 2	
	Time	Date	Goal	Actual	Goal	Actual	Goal	Actual	Goal	Actual	Goal	Actual
Time Trials												
Races												

Note: Although this is a grid of most meaningful time trial and racing distances, it is unlikely that you will fill out the entire chart in the course of a training and racing year.

the total runner's almanac

RACES – GOALS & ACTUALS

Date	Race	Times						Finish Place		Notes
		Average Pace		Finish						
		Goal	Actual	Goal	Actual	Goal	Actual	Goal	Actual	

Note: This can serve as an annual record of all races in one year, as a historical record of one particular race, or as a combination of the two.

the total runner's almanac

RACES – GOALS & ACTUALS

Date	Race	Times						Finish Place		Notes
		Average Pace		Finish						
		Goal	Actual	Goal	Actual		Goal	Actual		

Note: This can serve as an annual record of all races in one year, as a historical record of one particular race, or as a combination of the two.

RACES TO DO
a planning grid

Date	Name	Location	Distance	Course Type	Goal	Prize Purse	Notes

RACES TO DO
a planning grid

Date	Name	Location	Distance	Course Type	Goal	Prize Purse	Notes

RACE RECORD

Date	Race	Times									Total	Place	Notes
		Splits											

RACE RECORD

Date	Race	Times											Total	Place	Notes
		Splits													

SUMMARY TEMPLATES AND CHARTS – USAGE GUIDELINES

1. On the next two pages are two annual summaries. Please note that you may want to modify these summaries to, say, a ten-week period to match your training and racing schedule. The important point is to use these summaries to help you understand your *accumulated running load* and its effect on your training, racing and overall well-being! You have to pick the exact period you want to use for each "quarter" – it could be ten weeks, it could be 15 weeks or it could be the calendar quarter.

2. Following these two summaries is a chart grid with 26 x 54 squares, allowing for a plot with the weeks of one calendar year along the x-axis (horizontal axis) and distance (or time) along the y-axis.

3. One interesting exercise might be to transpose your running chart on top of your physiological value chart; a second one might be to plot in your race performances and correlate them with your other values.

4. When plotting, you may find a biweekly format more informative due to large weekly fluctuations in your running. Some runners prefer a monthly format.

ANNUAL SUMMARY – I

			Year			
		Quarter			Average	**Total**
					Weekly	Monthly	
Training Values	Run						
Physio-logical Values	Heart Rate	Morning					
		AT					
		Max					
	Weight						
	% Body Fat						

Note: This summary chart is somewhat "over-comprehensive." It is unlikely that you will find any real benefit from calculating all these averages and totals. Pick the ones that seem the most valuable and informative *to you*. AT is your anaerobic threshold.

the total runner's almanac

ANNUAL SUMMARY II

Run			Notes

Run			Notes
			TOTAL

ANNUAL CHART

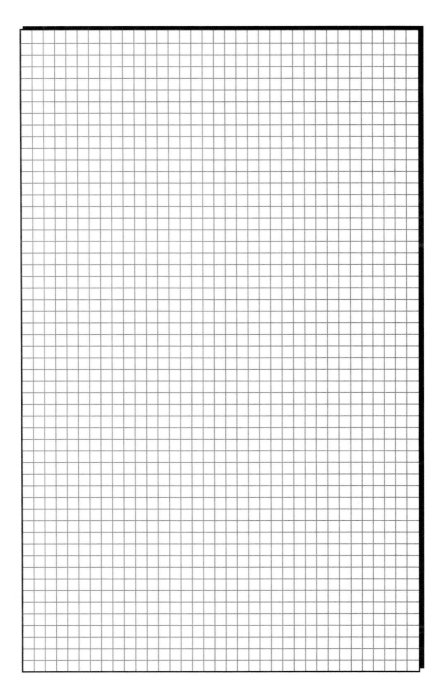

Note: Use this chart to plot your running values. You may gain even more insight by correlating these values *graphically* with your physiological values, race results, feeling of well-being and (let's hope, lack of) injuries.

the total runner's almanac

Conversion Charts & Figures

Runners on all sides of the many oceans on our globe are frustrated by the different, and seemingly meaningless, methods of measuring things. Though we are going towards one universal standard of measurement, there is still variety enough to befuddle even the most intelligent observer. Provided here, therefore, is a set of conversion figures. Add to this a calculator (or a pen and a paper) and grade school mathematics, and you're home free. (**It looks hairier than it is.**)

Warning: don't attempt to do these calculations in your head while racing!

US to Metric		
To Obtain	**Multiply**	**By**
meters	feet	0.3048
meters	yards	0.9144
kilometers	miles	1.609
kilometers/hour	miles/hour	1.609
grams	ounces	28.35
kilograms	pounds	0.4536
milliliters (cc)	fluid ounces	29.57
liters	gallons	3.785

Metric to US		
To Obtain	**Multiply**	**By**
feet	meters	3.281
yards	meters	1.094
miles	kilometers	0.6214
miles/hour	kilometers/hours	0.6214
ounces	grams	0.03527
pounds	kilograms	2.205
fluid ounces	milliliters (cc)	0.03381
gallons	liters	0.2642

Convert minutes per mile to kilometer pace

1. Convert minutes into seconds.
2. Multiply this figure by 0.6214.
3. Divide this figure by 60.
4. Subtract the integer portion.
5. Multiply the remaining fraction by 60.
6. Take the minutes from the integer portion in step 3 and the seconds from the integer portion in step 5.

Example: convert a 6:15 mile pace to a kilometer pace.
1. 6 x 60 + 15 = 360 + 15 = 375
2. 375 x 0.6214 = 233.03
3. 233.03/60 = 3.88
4. 3.88 - 3 = 0.88
5. 0.88 x 60 = 53.03
6. **3 min 53 sec, or 3:53 pace**

Convert kilometer pace to minutes per mile

1. Convert minutes into seconds.
2. Multiply this figure by 1.609.
3. Divide this figure by 60.
4. Subtract the integer portion.
5. Multiply the remaining fraction by 60.
6. Take the minutes from the integer portion in step 3 and the seconds from the integer portion in step 5.

Example: convert a 3:42 kilometer pace to a mile pace.
1. 3 x 60 + 42 = 180 + 42 = 222
2. 222 x 1.609 = 357.20
3. 357.20/60 = 5.95
4. 5.95 - 5 = 0.95
5. 0.95 x 60 = 57.20
6. **5 min 57 sec, or 5:57 pace**

ORDER FORM

Trimarket

2264 Bowdoin Street
Palo Alto, CA 94306
USA

Phone: 1-415-494-1406
Fax: 1-415-494-1413

E-mail: 70470.527@compuserve.com

Internet:
http://w3.one.net/~friweb
http://www.enduranceplus.com/trimarket

In the US, call toll free:
1-800-533-3644

International orders please submit an international money order drawn on a US bank.

Please send me the following:

____ each of the total runner's almanac at $12.95

____ each of the total fitness log at $9.95

____ each of finding the wheel's hub by Scott Tinley at $9.95

____ each of Can You Make a Living Doing That? by Brad Kearns at $9.95

____ each of the total triathlon almanac - 3 *(third edition)* at $16.95

____ each of the total triathlon almanac *(second edition)* at $16.95

____ each of the total triathlon almanac - 1993 *(first edition)* at $16.95

____ each of the video Strength Training for Total Body Fitness by Mark Allen and Paula Newby-Fraser with certified fitness specialist Diane Buchta at $29.95

In California, add 7.75% sales tax

Shipping, within USA $3.00 ($1.00 each additional)

Shipping, priority (or international) $5.00 ($2.00 each additional)

_____ **TOTAL**

I understand that I may return any unused book for a full refund if not satisfied.

Name: _____

Address: _____

the total runner's almanac

OTHER POPULAR TRIMARKET TITLES

the total fitness log

this new multifitness book has advice from top fitness authorities.

Includes sections on:

- cycling
- running
- walking
- nutrition
- swimming
- cross-training
- in-line skating
- mountain biking
- working out in the gym
- training with a heart rate monitor

$9.95

the total triathlon almanac -3

is the most detailed and comprehensive of all combined training logs and training handbooks. Specifically for the multisport athlete, this almanac is described by multiple Hawaii Ironman winner Mark Allen as, quote: "the best training manual and logbook on the market (and) Highly recommended."

$16.95

finding the wheel's hub
by Scott Tinley

One of triathlon's enduring legends, this Ironman Hall of Famer tells it all in this his third book. Described by running's Bill Rodgers as, quote: "Scott Tinley brings you into the intense eye of the triathlon, spelling it out clearly and with a potent sense of humor. I found this a fascinating book."

$9.95

Can You Make a Living Doing That?
by Brad Kearns

Mark Allen describes this book as, quote: "a refreshing departure from the common 'how to' books in sports. Brad goes beyond the race results and workout miles to provide an intimate look at the lifestyle of a professional athlete. I highly recommend this book from one of the most colorful personalities in sports today."

$9.95

Order form on reverse page

the total runner's almanac